D0630454

Hard Press

OCCASIONAL THOUGHTS

In reference to a

Vertuous or Christian

LIFE.

THE PREFACE.

The following discourse was written some Years since, not without the thought that, possibly, it might be of farther use than for the entertainment of the Writer: Yet so little express Intention was there of Publishing the Product of those leisure Hours it employ'd, that these Papers lay by for above two Years unread, and almost forgotten. After which time, being perus'd and Corrected, they were communicated to some Friends of the Authors, who judging them capable to be useful, they are now sent into the World in that Hope.

There is nothing pretended or suppos'd to be in them which is not obvious: but Truths the most evident, are sometimes overlook'd, or not sufficiently and universally attended to: And where these are Truths of moment, it is no ill Service, by frequent representations of them, to procure them attention.

I think there can be few heartily concerned for the Vice and Immorality that abounds amongst us, who have not sometimes reflected upon loose or careless Education, as one cause thereof: But yet the great weight that right Instruction and Discipline of Youth, is of, in respect both of Peoples present and future Felicity, is (as I take it) far from being generally so settl'd in the Minds of Parents, as to be steadily look'd upon by them as the one thing to that degree necessary, that without due care taken thereof, all other indeavours, to render their Children happy, either in this Life, or in that which is to come, are likely to be very inefficacious.

That right Instruction, in regard of Vertue, consists in joining together, inseparably, good Principles with early Habits, either of these being insufficient without the other, is likewise, I presume, no new Thought: But is yet what appears to me to be very little reflected upon. When this is duly consider'd, People cannot, I think, but be soon convinc'd from what Hands the right Instruction spoken of, ought to come; for nothing can, in my Opinion, be more obvious than that is. If these_ *occasional thoughts shall produce better digested ones from any other Hand; or shall themselves be any way serviceable to the reducing or directing of one single Soul into the paths of Vertue, I shall not repent the Publishing them: And however useless they may be to this end (sincerely aim'd at) yet the very Design will intitle them to no unfavourable reception: For but to indeavour to contribute, in the least degree, to the Honour of God, or Good of Mankind, can never stand in need of Pardon. And such a Modesty or Fear of displeasing any as withholds Men from enterprising the one, or the other of these, where nothing but their own Credit is hazarded, should the design not succeed, is, on the contrary, very blameable.*

Besides these two Motives, could I need any other to ingage me in the defence of Vertue, I should find yet a very powerful one in that dutiful Affection which I pay, and which every Subject ows to a_ *good Prince: Since the Queen, I am fully perswaded, would not so much rejoyce in the Accession of great Kingdoms to her Dominions, as to see the People, already happy in Her Government over them, indeavouring to make themselves and one another so, in following the great Example which She sets them of Vertue and Piety.*

4

*****

OCCASIONAL THOUGHTS

In reference to a

Vertuous or Christian

Life.

There is no so constant and satisfactory a Pleasure, to those who are capable of it, as Rational Conversation gives: And to me, depriv'd of that Enjoyment, the remembrance thereof, is, in my present Solitude, the most delightful Entertainment: Wherein some of my leisure hours will not, I hope, be mispent, should this engage me to prosecute such Thoughts as were lately suggested to me by others. The which taking their rise from a particular Enquiry, and thence proceeding to a general Consideration of the Folly and Madness of Rational Creature's acting, as if they had no other Principle to direct or determin them, than the Incitements of their Passions and Appetites, comprehended at once the unhappiness of Mankind, both Here and Hereafter. Since those Breaches of the Eternal Law of Reason, which disorder Common-wealths and Kingdoms; disturb the Peace of Families; and make by far the greatest part of the Private Infelicities of Particular Persons in this World, are what the Sovereign Disposer of all things has ordain'd, shall render Men miserable in a future Life also.

A survey of which Moral Irregularities, as bringing into view a large Scene of Human Depravity, does indeed furnish matter for melancholy, rather than pleasing Contemplations: But the Mind is sometimes no less affected with Delight, wherein there is a mixture of sadness on Subjects, which in themselves consider'd are ungrateful, than on occasions the most welcome to us: And such a just zeal in any for the interests of Vertue, as makes them, with a Charitable concern, reflect on the miscarriages of others, and thence take occasion to examine their own Actions by the true Rules and Measures of their Duty, expresses a disposition of Mind too becoming Rational Creatures, and too seldom met withal, not to please, tho' excited by Representations which are disagreeable; provided they are of such a matter as is not then new to our Thoughts.

That the Gross of Mankind do every where live in opposition to that Rule of Nature which they ought to obey, is a sad Truth; but that we who have this Rule enforc'd by a clearer Light, are included herein, and do in this find the source of many Evils, not only fear'd, but which we actually feel, are Considerations yet more affecting, and not a little aggravated in that, within Memory, this heretofore sober Nation has been debauch'd from Principles of Vertue and Religion, to such an excess of Vice and Prophaneness, that it has been Fashionable to have no shame of the grossest Immoralities; and Men have thought even to recommend themseves by avow'd Impiety. A Change which could not be consider'd without extream regret by all who either were in earnest Christians, or who truly lov'd the Prosperity of their Country: And as upon this occasion there was reason to be sensible that nothing operates so powerfully as the example of Princes; some have been of later Years induc'd to hope for a revolution in our Manners, no less advantageous than what has hitherto secur'd those Civil and Religious Liberties, without which it is impossible for Vertue to subsist among any People whatsoever. But Experience shows that Humane Nature is much easier led into Evil, than reduc'd from it; and that inveterate Maladies are difficultly cur'd.

When Men's Practices have infected their Principles and Opinions; and these have had time again reciprocally to confirm them in their Vicious Habits and Customs, the whole Constitution is corrupted; and the Personal Vertue then of the Prince (however conspicuous) will not, without a concurrence of other means, influence farther than to make (it may be) some change in the Garb, or Fashion of Men's Vices.

A due and vigorous Execution of proper Laws against Immorality and Prophaneness, is that alone which will effectually restrain them: And a right care had of Education, is the only humane means of making People truly Vertuous. Whenever our inferiour Magistrates shall be such as will be *a terror to Evil doers, and encouragers of those who do well,* and when Parents shall be perswaded that it is in their power to procure to their Children more valuable Treasures than Riches and Honours; the ancient Vertue of our Ancestors will then quickly be equall'd, if not surpass'd, by that of their Posterity: But till then, it is in vain to expect that any great Advances should be made towards an Amendment, as necessary to our present and National, as to our Personal and Future Happiness.

What the force of Education is upon our Minds, and how by a due regard had to it, Common-wealths and Kingdoms have flourished, and become famous; and how much this has been recommended by Wise Men in all Ages, requires but a small consideration of Humane Nature, and Acquaintance with History to inform us; nor is any thing more obvious to observe than the power of Education. This matter yet has no where been ordinarily look'd after, proportionably to the moment it is visibly of: And even the most sollicitous about it, have usually employ'd their care herein but by halves with respect to the Principal Part in so great a concernment; for the information and improvement of the Understanding by useful Knowledge, (a thing highly necessary to the right regulation of the Manners) is commonly very little thought of in reference to one whole Sex; even by those who in regard of the other, take due care hereof. But to this omission in respect of one Sex, it is manifestly very much to be attributed, that that pains which is often bestow'd upon the other, does so frequently, as it does, prove ineffectual: Since the actual assistance of Mothers, will (generally speaking) be found necessary to the right forming of the Minds of their Children of both Sexes; and the Impressions receiv'd in that tender Age, which is unavoidably much of it passed among Women, are of exceeding consequence to Men throughout the whole remainder of their Lives, as having a strong and oftentimes unalterable influence upon their future Inclinations and Passions.

As those Persons who afforded that agreeable Conversation I have mention'd, were the greater part of them Ladies, it was not strange if they express'd much displeasure at the too general neglect of the Instruction of their Sex; a Reflection not easily to be avoided by them, when their thoughts upon the miscarriages and unhappiness of Mankind in general, terminated in a more peculiar Consideration of that part which those of their own Condition had in the one, and the other. Wherein the Conversation concluded where it had begun; the occasion which introduced it having

8

been the Enquiry of a Lady, What was the Opinion of one in the Company concerning a Book Intitled *Conseils d'Ariste sur les Moyens de conserver sa Reputation*? Of which (she said) she had heard divers Persons of Merit and Quality, speak very differently: Some as if it contained the most useful Instructions that could be given for the rendring any young Lady such as her best Friends could wish she should be; and others, as relishing too much of an Antiquated severity, not indulgent enough either to the natural and agreeable Gaiety of Youth, or to that innocent Liberty now in use, deriv'd like most of our other Fashions, from that Nation where these *Counsels* were thought needful.

I remember not the Book you speak of enough to answer to your desire, (reply'd the Person to whom this Enquiry was address'd) but what you say is objected to these *Conseils* is without doubt impertinent, unless the Precepts therein meant to be condemn'd, are shown to be in themselves faulty; it being certainly otherwise no matter of exception to them that they are not Indulgent to what an Age, the Manners whereof they were intended to correct, had establish'd or found agreeable. This Objection yet can hardly (I think) be less just, than such a Character of any Book of this Nature, as some it seems give of this: the Author whereof pretended not (as I suppose) to so much in his Design, as these People find in his Performance. And the nature and extent of a Christian's Duty is but little in their thoughts, who think that any Rules dictated by Prudence, or Experience of the World, and directed to the Glory of a good Name, are such Instructions as can render any one what they ought to be. A *solid Vertue* can alone do this; the Possession whereof is infinitely preferable to that of Reputation; with which yet it is so rarely unattended, that one may affirm there is no so secure and easie a way (especially for a Lady) to acquire and conserve the Reputation of being Vertuous, as really to be so.

But Vertue is not (tho often so misrepresented) included in Innocency; or does consist in a partial Practice of Actions praiseworthy; for its extent is equal to our liberty of Action; and its Principle the most Active one of the Mind; Vertue being the natural result of a sincere desire to conform in all things to the Law set us by our Maker; which who so truly endeavours, will not find much occasion for such kind of Advices as the above-mentioned ones, either to correct their Faults, or teach them to put a mask over them; an ill use sometimes made of this sort of Instructions: However a better might be, since it is true, that young People from the Experience of others may learn many things in reference to their Conduct, the knowledge whereof they would buy too dear at their own. The difficulty yet that there is in applying general Rules to particular Cases, makes (I presume) Books of this sort, how good soever in the kind, of less advantage to those who most need them, than some imagine them to be.

This which was then said on the Subject of these *Conseils* (lying by accident in the way) suggests to me now two things, wherein the Documents ordinarily given to such young Ladies, as are intended to have the best care taken of their Instruction, are, I think, very defective; and the fitter to be redress'd, as being of peculiar ill consequence in a Sceptical, loose and unthinking Age; wherein Wit is apt to pass upon many for Reason.

The first of these is, That those Notions, or Ideas of Vertue, and consequent Rules of Action, which are usually given to such young Persons, do rarely carry along with them an entire conviction of their Truth and Reasonableness: Whence if these Instructions at any time happen strongly to cross the Inclinations of those to whom they are given, it will appear rational to question their Solidity: And when Principles that thwart People's passions or interests, come once to be doubted of by them, it is great odds, that they will sooner be slighted, than better examin'd.

Now, this want of apparent Truth and Reasonableness, is not only where the *Notions* and *Precepts* giv'n, are in themselves such as either in Whole, or in Part, are not True or Rational; but also (oftentimes) where they are altogether conformable to right Reason: In which cases, the want of apparent Reasonableness, proceeds from a defect of such Antecedent Knowledge in those who are design'd to be instructed, as is necessary to the seeing their Reasonableness of the Instructions giv'n them; that is to say, To their discerning the conformity with, or evident deduction of such Instructions from some Truths which are unquestion'd by them: the which should be the Principles of True Religion, so clearly made out to them, as to be by them acknowledg'd for Verities. Religion being (as I shall take it at present for granted) the only sufficient ground or solid support of Vertue; For the belief of a Superior, Omnipotent Being, inspecting our Actions, and who will Reward or Punish us accordingly, is in all Men's Apprehensions the strangest, and in truth the only stable and irresistible Argument for submitting our Desires to a constant Regulation, wherein it is that Vertue does consist.

How far Natural Religion alone is sufficient for this, is very fit to be consider'd: But I conclude that among us, there are few who pretend to recommend Vertue, but who do so either with no respect at all to Religion, and upon Principles purely Humane, or else with reference to the Christian Religion. The first of these, it is already said, will be ineffectual; and it is no less certain that the Christian Religion cannot be a solid Foundation for Vertue, where Vertue being inculcated upon the Declarations of the Gospel, those who are thus instructed, are not convinc'd of the Authority and Evidence of that Revelation; which but too commonly is the Case: Instructors, instead of Teaching this necessary previous Knowledge of Religion, generally, supposing it to be already in them whom they instruct, who in reality neither have it, or have ever been so before-hand Taught, as to make it a reasonable Presumption that they should have it. Whence all the Endeavours of making them Vertuous in consequence of their Christianity, are but attempting to raise a real Superstructure upon an only imaginary Foundation; for Truths receiv'd upon any other Ground than their own Evidence, tho' they may, perhaps, find entertainment, yet will never gain to themselves a sure hold upon the Mind; and so soon as they become troublesome, are in great danger of being question'd; whereby whatever is Built upon them, must be likewise liable to be suspected for fallacious: And however empty Declamations do often-times make livelier impressions upon Young People than substantial Reasoning, yet these impressions are, for the most part, easily effac'd; and especially are so out of their Minds who naturally are the capablest of right Reason; as among other instances appears in this, that prophane Wits do often even railly Women of the Best Parts (Religiously Bred as they call it) out of their Duty: These not seeing (as they should have been early Taught to do) that what they have learn'd to be their

Duty is not grounded upon the uncertain and variable Opinion of Men, but the unchangeable nature of things; and has an indissolvable Connection with their Happiness or Misery.

Now those who have the Direction of Young Ladies in their Youth, so soon as past Child-hood, whether they be the Parents, Governesses, or others, do not, most commonly, neglect the Teaching them That which is the Ground and Support of all the Good Precepts they give them; because that Principles of Religion are by them believed to be unnecessary; or are not in their Thoughts; but because they presume, as has been said, that those now under their Care are already sufficiently instructed herein; *viz.* When their Nurses, or Maids, Taught them their Catechisms; that is to say, Certain Answers to a Train of Questions adapted to some approv'd System of Divinity.

That this is sufficient Instruction in Religion, is apparently a Belief pretty general: And not only such Young Ladies as have newly put off their Bibs and Aprons, but even the greatest Number of their Parents, and Teachers themselves, would, yet less than They, be pleas'd if one should tell them that those who know so much as this, may nevertheless be very Ignorant concerning the Christian Religion; these Old People no more than the Young Ones, being able to give any farther Account thereof than they have thus been taught. It is yet true that many who have Learn'd, and who well remember long Catechisms, with all their pretended Proofs, are so far from having that Knowledge which Rational Creatures ought to have of a Religion they profess to Believe they can only be Sav'd by, as that they are not able to say, either what this Religion does Consist in, or why it is they Believe it; and are so little instructed by their Catechisms, as that, oftentimes, they understand not so much as the very Terms they have Learn'd in them: And more often find the Proportions therein contain'd, so short in the Information of their Ignorance; or so unintelligible, to their Apprehensions; or so plainly contradictory of the most obvious Dictates of common Sense; that Religion (for the which they never think of looking beyond these Systems) appears to them indeed a thing not Built upon, or defensible by Reason: In consequence of which Opinion, the weakest attaques made against it, must needs render such Persons (at the least) wavering in their Belief of it; Whence those Precepts of Vertue, which they have receiv'd as bottom'd thereon, are, in a Time wherein Scepticism and Vice, pass for Wit and Gallantry, necessarily brought under the suspicion of having no solid Foundation; and the recommenders thereof, either of Ignorance, or Artifice.

But the not making Young People understand their Religion, is a fault not peculiar in regard to the instruction of one Sex alone, any otherwise than as consider'd in its Consequences; whereby (ordinarily speaking) Women do the most inevitably suffer; as not having the like Advantage (at least early enough) of Correcting the Ignorance, or Errors of their Child-hood that Men have.

The other thing which I imagine faulty, does more peculiarly concern the Sex, but is yet chiefly practic'd in regard of Those of it who are of Quality, and that is, the insinuating into them such a Notion of Honour as if the praise of Men ought to be the

Supreme Object of their Desires, and the great Motive with them to Vertue: *A Term* which when apply'd to Women, is rarely design'd, by some People, to signifie any thing but the single Vertue of Chastity; the having whereof does with no more Reason intitle a Lady to the being thought such as she should be in respect of Vertue, than a handsome Face, unaccompany'd by other Graces, can render her Person truly Amiable. Or rather, *Chastity* is so essential to, singly, so small a part of the Merit of a Beautiful Mind, that it is better compar'd to Health, or Youth, in the Body, which alone have small Attractions, but without which all other Beauties are of no Value.

To perswade Ladies then that what they cannot want without being contemptible, is the chief Merit they are capable of having, must naturally either give them such low thoughts of themselves as will hinder them from aspiring after any thing Excellent, or else make them believe that this mean Opinion of them is owing to the injustice of such Men in their regard as pretend to be their Masters. A belief too often endeavour'd to be improv'd in them by others.

But whether any Natural, or Design'd ill consequence follow from hence or no, this is certain, that a true Vertue is the best Security against all the Misfortunes that can be fear'd, and the surest Pledge of all the Comforts that can be hop'd for in a Wife, *viz.* such a Vertue whose Foundation is a desire above all things, of approving our selves to God; the most opposite Principle whereunto is the making the Esteem of Men the chief End, and Aim of our Actions; as it is propos'd to be of Their's who have the empty Idea of Glory set before them as the great Motive to, and high Reward of that particular Duty, which (as if it included all others) does ordinarily ingross the Name of Vertue, with regard to Women. A very wrong Motive this, to Those who aim at what is truely Honourable, and such as may (and often does) as well produce an ill, as a good effect.

But these wrong or partial Notions of Vertue, and Honour, are the Product only of such Men's Inventions as are unwilling to regulate their own Actions by the Universal, and Eternal Law of Right; and therefore are ever desirous to find out such Rules for other People, as will not reach themselves, and as they can extend and contract as they please. In saying of which, it is not deny'd, that the love of Praise may be sometimes usefully instill'd into very Young Persons, to give them the desire of Eminence in things wherein they should endeavour to excel: But as this ought never to be made the incitement to any Vertue but in the earliest Childhood of our Reason, so also at no time should Glory (which is the Reward only of Actions transcendently Good, either in kind, or degree) be represented as the purchase of barely not meriting Infamy: The apprehension of which, is a much stronger perswasive to most People not to do amiss, than that of Glory, which cannot consist with it: For no Body can rationally think that Glory can be due to them for doing that, which it would be shameful in them not to do. But there is yet a farther Folly and ill Consequence in Men's intitling Ladies to Glory on account of Chastity which is, that the conceit hereof (especially in those who are Beautiful) does ordinarily produce in them a Pride and Imperiousness, that is very troublesome to such as are the most concern'd in them.

12

One whose business it was to remark the Humours of the Age, and of Mankind in general, has, I remember, made a Husband on this occasion to say,

> *Such Vertue is the Plague of Human Life,*
> *A Vertuous Woman, but a Cursed Wife.*

And he adds,

In Unchaste Wives, There's yet a kind of recompencing Ease, Vice keeps 'em Humble, gives 'em care to please. But against clamorous Vertue, what Defence?

If Mr. *Dryden* did distinguish herein, between real Vertue and that Idol one of Men's Invention, he was, perhaps, not much in the wrong in what he suggests: But if he design'd in this a Satyr against Marriage, as a state in the which a Man can no way be happy, it appears then how much Vertue is prejudiced by this foreign Support, whilst it becomes thereby expos'd to such a Censure; which if it may be Just in reference to a vain Glorious Chastity, yet can never be so of a truly Vertuous one: Obedience to the Law of God, being an Universal Principle, and admitting of no Irregularity in one thing any more than in another, which falls under it's Direction.

It is indeed only a Rational Fear of God, and desire to approve our selves to him, that will teach us in All things, uniformly to live as becomes our Reasonable Nature; to inable us to do which, must needs be the great Business and End of a Religion which comes from God.

But how differently from this has the Christian Religion been represented by those who place it in useless Speculations, Empty Forms, or Superstitious Performances? The Natural Tendency of which things being to perswade Men that they may please God at a cheaper Rate than by the Denial of their Appetites, and the Mortifying of their Irregular Affections, these Misrepresentations of a pretended Divine Revelation have been highly prejudicial to Morality: And, thereby, been also a great occasion of Scepticism; for the Obligation to Vertue being loosen'd, Men easily become Vicious; which when once they are, the Remorse of their Consciences bringing them to desire that there should be no future Reckoning for their Actions; and even that there should be no God to take any cognizance of them; they often come (in some degree at least) to be perswaded both of the one, and the other of these. And thus, many times, there are but a few steps between a Zealous Bigot, and an Infidel to all Religion.

Scepticism, or rather *Infidelity,* is the proper Disease our Age, and has proceeded from divers Causes: But be the remoter or original ones what they will, it could never have prevail'd as it has done, had not Parents very generally contributed thereto, either her by negligence of their Children's Instruction; or Instructing them very ill in respect of Religion.

It might indeed seem strange to one who had no experience of Mankind, that People (however neglected in their Education) could, when they came to years of Judgment, be to such a degree wanting to themselves, as not to seek right Information concerning Truths of so great Moment to them not to be Ignorant of, or mistaken in, as are those of Religion. Yet such is the wretched Inconsideration Natural to most Men, that (in fact) it is no uncommon thing at all to see Men live day after day, in the pursuit of their Inclinations, without ever exerting their Reason to any other purpose than the gratification of their Passions; and no wonder can it then be if they give in to the belief, or take up with a blind Perswasion of such Opinions as they see to be most in Credit; and which will also the best suit their turn?

Absolute Atheism does no doubt the best serve Their's, who live as if there was no God in the World; but how far so great Non-sense as this, has been able to obtain, is not easie to say: downright Atheism being what but few Men will own. To me it appears (in that Those who will expose themselves to argue against the Existence of a God, do rarely venture to produce any Hypothesis of their own to be fairly examin'd and compar'd with that which they reject: But that their opposition to a Deity, consists only in Objections which may as well be retorted upon themselves, and which at best prove nothing but the shortness of Humane Understanding) to me, I say, it appears from hence probable that the greatest part of Atheistick Reasoners, do rather desire, and seek to be Atheists, than that in reality they are so. Men, who are accustom'd to Believe without any Evidence of Reason for what they Believe, are, it is likely, more in earnest in this wild Opinion: And in all appearance very many there are among us of such as a Learned Man calls *Enthusiastick Atheists, viz.* who deny the Existence of an Invisible, Omniscient, Omnipotent, first Cause of all things, only through a certain Sottish disbelief of whatsoever they cannot either see or feel; never consulting their Reason in the Case. That there are some who do thus, their Discourses assure us: The Actions of many others, are unaccountable without supposing them to be of this Number; and it is very suspicious that to this Atheism as to a secret Cause thereof, may be attributed the avow'd Averseness of many Men to reveal'd Religion, since in a Country where People are permitted to read the Scriptures, and to use their Reason freely in matters of Religion; and where, in effect, there are so many Rational Christians, 'tis hard to conceive that Men can be long Scepticks in regard of Christianity, if they are indeed hearty Deists; and fully perswaded of the Truths of Natural Religion.

But it being sufficiently obvious that want of Instruction concerning Religion does in a Sceptical Age dispose Men to Scepticism and Infidelity, which often terminates in downright Atheism; let us see whether, or no, Ill, by which I mean, all irrational Instruction in regard of Religion, has not the same Tendency.

It is as undeniable as the difference between Men's being in, and out of their Wits, that Reason ought to be to Rational Creatures the Guide of their Belief: That is to say, That their Assent to any thing, ought to be govern'd by that proof of its Truth, whereof Reason is the Judge; be it either Argument, or Authority, for in both Cases Reason must determine our Assent according to the validity of the Ground it finds it Built on: By Reason being here understood that Faculty in us which discovers, by the intervention of intermediate Ideas, what Connection Those in the Proposition have one with another: Whether *certain*; *probable*; or *none at all*; according whereunto, we ought to regulate our Assent. If we do not so, we degrade our selves from being Rational Creatures; and deprive our selves of the only Guide God has given us for our Conduct in our Actions and Opinions.

Authority yet is not hereby so subjected to Reason, as that a Proposition which we see not the Truth of, may not nevertheless be Rationally assented to by us.

For tho' Reason cannot from the Evidence of the thing it self induce our assent to any Proposition, where we cannot perceive the Connexion of the Ideas therein contain'd; yet if it appears that such a Proposition was truly reveal'd by God, nothing can be more Rational than to believe it: since we know that God can neither Deceive, nor be Deceived: That there are Truths above our Conception, and that God may (if he so pleases) communicate these to us by Supernatural Revelation.

The part of Reason then, in regard of such a Proposition as this, is, only to examine whether it be indeed a Divine Revelation: which should Reason not attest to the Truth of; it is then evidently Irrational to give, or require assent to it as being so.

And as plainly Irrational must it be to give, or require assent to any thing as a Divine Revelation, which is evidently contrary to Reason; no less being herein imply'd than that God has made us so as to see clearly that to be a Truth, which is yet a Falshood; the which, were it so, would make the Testimony of our Reason useless to us; and thereby destroy also the Credit of all Revelation; for no stronger proof can be had of the Truth of any Revelation than the Evidence of our Reason that it is a Revelation.

Now if the Christian Religion be very often represented as teaching Doctrines clearly contrary to Reason; or as exacting belief of what we can neither perceive the Truth of, nor do find to be reveal'd by Christ, or his Apostles: And, (what is still more) that this pretended Divine Religion does even consist in such a Belief as This; so that a Man cannot be a Christian without believing what he neither from Arguments or Authority has any Ground for believing; what must the Natural Consequence of this be upon all whoever so little consult their Reason, when in riper Years they come to reflect hereupon, but to make them recal, and suspend, at least, their assent to the Truth of a Religion that appears to them thus Irrational? since an Irrational Religion can never Rationally be conceived to come from God.

And if Men once come to call in question such Doctrines as (tho' but upon slender Grounds for it) they had received for unquestionable Truths of Religion, they are ordinarily more likely to continue Scepticks, or to proceed to an intire disbelief of this Religion, than to take occasion from hence to make a just search after its Verity: The want either of Capacity, Leisure or Inclination for such an inquiry, disposing Men, very generally, to neglect it; and easily to satisfy themselves in so doing, from a perswasion that the Christian Religion is indeed self condemn'd: Those whom they imagine to have understood it as well as any Men, having never taught them that this Religion does so much as pretend to any Foundation in, or appeal to Reason, that Faculty in us which distinguishes us from Beasts, and the Actual use thereof from Mad-Men; but indeed Taught them the contrary: And thus prejudg'd, it truly is that the Christian Religion, by those who disbelieve it, has usually come to be rejected; without ever having been allow'd a fair Examination.

From what has been said, I think it does appear, that Ill, that is to say, Irrational Instruction concerning Religion, as well as want of Instruction, disposes to Scepticism: And this being so, what wonder can it be that Scepticism having once become fashionable, should continue so? the un-instructed, and the ill-instructed, making by so great odds, the Majority. For Those who have no Religion themselves, do not often take care that others should have any: And They who adhere to a misgrounded Perswasion concerning Religion, retaining a Reverence for their Teachers, do, in consequence thereof, commonly presume that their Children cannot be better taught than they have been before them; which is generally (as has been said) only by the learning of some approved Catechism; wherein, commonly enough, the first principles of Religion are not, as they should be, laid down, but suppos'd: and from whence Those who learn them, learn nothing except that certain Propositions are requir'd to be Believed, which perhaps, they find inconceivable by them; or (at best) whereof they see neither use, nor certainty: These Catechisms yet being represented to Children by those whom they the most Esteem, and Credit, as containing Sacred verities on the Belief of which Salvation does depend, they quickly become afraid to own that they are not convinc'd of the Truth of what is deliver'd in them: For the greater part among our selves are instructed in Religion much after the same manner that that good Lady of the Church of *Rome* instructed her Child; who when the Girl told her, she *could not believe Transubstantiation*; Reply'd, *What? You do you not believe Transubstantiation? You are a naughty Girl, and must be whip'd.*

Instead of having their reasonable Inquiries satisfy'd, and incourag'd, Children are ordinarily rebuk'd for making any: from whence not daring in a short time to question any thing that is taught them in reference to Religion; they, (as the Girl above-mention'd was) are brought to say, that they *do Believe* whatever their Teachers tell them they must Believe; whilst in Truth they remain in an ignorant unbelief, which exposes them to be seduc'd by the most pitiful Arguments of the Atheistical, or of such as are disbelievers of reveal'd Religion.

The Foundation of All Religion is the belief of a God; or of a Maker and Governour of the World; the evidence of which, being visible in every thing; and the general Profession having usually stamp'd it with awe upon Children's Minds, they ought perhaps most commonly to be suppos'd to Believe This, rather than have doubts rais'd in them by going about to prove it to them: because those who are uncapable of long deductions of Reason, or attending to a train of Arguments, not finding the force thereof when offer'd to prove what they had always taken for a clear, and obvious verity, would be rather taught thereby to suspect that a Truth which they had hitherto look'd on as unquestionable, might rationally be doubted of, than be any ways confirm'd in the belief of it. But if any doubts concerning the Existence of God, do arise in their Minds, when they own this, or that this, can be discover'd by discoursing with them: such doubts should always be endeavour'd to be remov'd by the most solid Arguments of which Children are capable. Nor should They ever be rebuk'd for having those doubts; since not giving leave to look into the grounds of asserting any Truth, whatever it be, can never be the way to establish that Truth in any rational Mind; but, on the contrary, must be very likely to raise a suspicion that it is not well grounded.

The belief of a Deity being entertain'd; what should be first taught us should be what we are in the first place concern'd to know.

Now it is certain that what we are in the first place concern'd to know, is that which is necessary to our Salvation; and it is as certain that whatever God has made necessary to our Salvation, we are at the same time capable of knowing. All Instruction therefore which obtrudes upon any one as necessary to their Salvation, what they cannot understand or see the evidence of, is to that Person, wrong Instruction; and when any such unintelligible, or unevident Propositions are deliver'd to Children as if they were so visible Truths that a reason, or proof of them was not to be demanded by them, what effect can this produce in their Minds but to teach them betimes to silence and suppress their Reason; from whence they have afterwards no Principle of Vertue left; and their practices, as well as opinions, must needs (as is the usual consequence hereof) become expos'd to the Conduct of their own, or other Men's Fancies?

The existence of God being acknowledg'd a Truth so early receiv'd by us, and so evident to our Reason, that it looks like Natural Inscription; the Authority of that Revelation by which God has made known his Will to Men, is to be firmly establish'd in People's Minds upon its clearest, and most rational evidence; and consequentially They are then to be refer'd to the Scriptures themselves, to see therein what it is that God requires of them to *believe* and *to do*; the great Obligation they are under diligently to study these Divine Oracles being duly represented to them. But to exhort any one to search the Scriptures to the end of seeing therein what God requires of him, before he is satisfy'd that the Scriptures are a Revelation from God, cannot be rational: since any ones saying that the Scriptures are God's Word, cannot satisfy a rational and inquisitive Mind that they are so: and that the Books of the Old and New Testament were dictated by the Spirit of God, is not a self evident Proposition, but a Truth that demands to be made out, before it can be rationally assented to.

It should also be effectually Taught, and not in Words alone, That it is our Duty to study and examine the Scriptures, to the end of seeing therein what God requires of us to *believe*, and to *do*. But none are effectually, or sincerely taught this, if notwithstanding that this is sometimes told them, they are yet not left at liberty to believe, or not believe, according to what, upon examination, appears to them to be the sense of the Scriptures: for if we must not receive them in that sense, which, after our best inquiry, appears to us to be their meaning, it is visible that it signifies nothing to bid us search, and examine them.

These two things, *viz.* a rational assurance of the Divine Authority of the Scriptures, and a liberty of fairly examining them, are absolutely necessary to the satisfaction of any rational Person, concerning the certainty of the Christian Religion, and what it is that this Religion does consist in: and He who when he comes to be a Man, shall remember that being a Boy he has been check'd for doubting, instead of being better inform'd when he demanded farther proof than had been given him of the Divine Authority of the Scriptures: or that he has been reprehended for thinking that the Word of God contradicted some Article of his Catechism; has just ground, when he reflects thereupon, to question, whether or no, the Interaction of his Childhood has not been an Imposition upon his Reason; which he will no doubt be apt to believe the more, when others shall confidently affirm to him that it has been so: And in that Age of Men's Lives when they are in the eagerest pursuit of Pleasure, it is great odds (as has been already observ'd) that if, in regard of Religion, they come to lose the belief of what they have once thought unquestionable, they will more often be perswaded that there is no Truth at all therein, than set themselves seriously to find out what is so.

How dangerous a thing then is such Instruction in Religion, as teaches nothing unless it be to stifle the Suggestions of our Natural Light? But that such Instruction as this, is all that the far greatest Number of People have, there is too much ground to conclude, from the visible Ignorance even of the most of Those who are Zealous in some Profession of Christian Faith, and Worship: Few of These not being at a loss to answer, if ask'd, either, *What the Faith of a Christian does consist in?* Or, *Why they believe such Articles concerning it, as they profess to believe?*

That their God-fathers, and God-mothers ingag'd for them that they should believe so; is a reason for their doing it that I suppose, there are but Few who would not be asham'd to give; as seeing that a *Mahumetan* could not be thought to assert his Faith more absurdly in the Opinion of any indifferent By-stander, and yet it is evident that no better a reason than this have very many for their Belief.

What is the chief and highest end of Man? is a Question which, methinks, supposes the resolution of more antecedent Questions, than Children, untaught, can be presum'd to be resolv'd in. But be this Question ever so proper to begin a Catechism withal, the answer hereto, *viz. That Man's chief and highest end is to glorifie God, and enjoy him for ever*; is not surely very instructive of an ignorant Child. It is a good Question in the same Catechism; *How doth it appear the Scriptures are the Word of God?* But who would imagine that for the information of any one who wanted to be inform'd herein, it should be answer'd, *That the Scriptures manifest themselves to be the Word of God by their Majesty and Purity: by the consent of all the Parts, and by the scope of the whole; which is to give all Glory to God: by their Light and Power to convince, and convert Sinners; to comfort and build up Believers to Salvation: But the Spirit of God bearing Witness by and with the Scriptures, in the Heart of Man is alone able fully to perswade that they are the very Word of God.* One would almost be tempted to suspect that Men who talk'd thus, were not themselves thorowly perswaded that the Scriptures were indeed the Word of God; for how is it possible not only for a Young Boy, or Girl, but even for an *Indian* Man, or Woman, to be by this answer more convinc'd than they were before, of the Scriptures being what they are pretended to be? To assure any rational inquirer of Which, it is necessary they should be satisfied, That the Scriptures were indeed written by those whose Names they bear; That these Persons were unquestionable Witnesses, and Faithful Historians of the matters they relate; and that they had such a Guidance, and Direction from the Spirit of God as led them to deliver all necessary Truth, and to preserve them from all error prejudicial thereunto: which Things have so good evidence, that none who are not manifestly prejudic'd, can refuse assent thereto, when they are duly represented to them: but without having weigh'd this evidence, the Divine Authority of the Scriptures may, possibly, be by some firmly believ'd, but cannot be so upon the conviction of their Reason.

The Instruction then of most Peoples Younger Years being such as we have seen in regard of Religion: and *Vertue, viz.* The right regulation of our Passions, and Appetites, having (as has been abovesaid) no other sufficient inforcement than the Truths of Religion; can it reasonably be thought strange, that there is so little Vertue in the World as we find there is? or that correspondently to their Principles, Peoples Actions generally are (at best) unaccountable to their Reason? For Time, and more Years, if they give strength to our Judgments whereby we may be thought able to inform our selves, and correct the errors and defects of our Education, give also strength to our Passions; which grown strong, do furnish and suggest Principles suited to the purposes and ends that they propose; besides, that Ill Habits once settl'd, are hardly chang'd by the force of any principles of which Reason may come to convince Men at their riper Age: A Truth very little weigh'd; tho' nothing ought more to be so with respect to a vertuous Education; since rational Religion, so soon as they are capable thereof, is not more necessary to the ingaging People to Vertue, than is the fixing, and establishing in them good Habits betimes, even before they are capable of knowing any other reason for what they are taught to do, than that it is the Will of Those who have a just power over them that they should do so. For as without a Knowledge of the Truths of Religion, we should want very often sufficient Motives, and Encouragements to submit our Passions and Appetites to the Government of Reason; so without early Habits establish'd of denying our Appetites, and restraining our Inclinations, the Truths of Religion will operate but upon a very few, so far as they ought to do.

By Religion I understand still *Reveal'd Religion.* For tho' without the help of Revelation, the Commands of Jesus Christ (two positive Institutions only excepted) are, as dictates likewise of Nature, discoverable by the Light of Reason; and are no less the Law of God to rational Creatures than the injunctions of Revelation are; yet few would actually discern this Law of Nature in its full extent, meerly by the Light of Nature; or if they did, would find the inforcement thereof a sufficient Ballance to that Natural love of present pleasure which often opposes our compliance therewith; since before we come to such a ripeness of understanding as to be capable by unassisted Reason to discover from the Nature of Things the just measures of our Actions, together with the obligations we are under to comply therewithal; an evil indulgence of our Inclinations has commonly establish'd Habits in us too strong to be over-rul'd by the Force of Arguments; especially where they are not of very obvious deduction. Whence it may justly be infer'd that the Christian Religion is the alone Universally adapted means of making Men truly Vertuous; the *Law of Reason, or the Eternal Rule of Rectitude* being in the Word of God only, to those of all capacities, plainly, and Authoritatively deliver'd as the Law of God, duly inforc'd by Rewards and Punishments.

Yet in that Conformity with, and necessary support which our Religion brings to the Law of Reason, or Nature, that is to say, to Those dictates which are the result of the determinate and unchangeable Constitution of things (and which as being discoverable to us by our rational Faculties, are therefore sometimes call'd the Law of Reason, as well as the Law of Nature) Christianity does most conspicuously and evidently appear to be a Divine Religion; *viz.* to be from the Author of Nature; however incongruous some Men may phancy it to be for God supernaturally to reveal to Men what is naturally discoverable to them, by those Faculties he has given them: The which conceit together with not considering, or rightly weighing the inforcements which Natural Religion needs, and receives from Revelation, has very much dispos'd many to reject reveal'd Religion. Whereunto such Notions of Christianity as agree not to the Attributes of an Infinitely Wise and Good Being, which Reason teaches the first cause of all things to be, have also not a little contributed; for from hence many Men, zealous for the Honour of God and lovers of Mankind, have been prejudic'd against the Truth of the Christian Religion: In consequence whereof they have reasonably concluded that there was no such thing as reveal'd Religion; and from thence have again infer'd that Men had no need thereof to the Ends of Natural Religion.

Those yet who think Revelation to be needless in this regard, how well soever they may, possibly, intend to Natural Religion, do herein entertain an Opinion that would undermine it: Experience shewing us that Natural Light, unassisted by Revelation, is insufficent to the Ends of Natural Religion: A Truth necessary to be acknowledg'd to the having a due value for the benefit that we receive by the Revelation of Jesus Christ; and many, who profess belief in him, have not a right estimation of that benefit on this very account, *viz.* as thinking too highly, or rather wrongly of Natural Light: notwithstanding that nothing is more undeniably true than that from the meer Light of Nature Men actually were so far from discovering the Law of Nature in its full extent or force, as that they did not generally own, and but very imperfectly discern, its prescriptions or obligation. 'Tis also alike evident that as Christianity has prevail'd, it has together with Polytheism, and (in great measure) Idolatry, beaten out likewise the allow'd Practice of gross Immorality; which in the Heathen World was countenanc'd, and incourag'd by the examples of their very Gods themselves; and by being frequently made even a part in Religious Worship. For the Truth of this effect of Christianity we must appeal to History; from whence if any one should imagine they could oppose any contrary example, it could (I think) be taken but from one only Country; wherein (if the Historian says right) Morality was more exemplary than in any other that we know of for near 400 Years that its Pagan Natives possess'd it; whose exterminators (calling themselves Christians) made it a most deplorable Scene of Injustice, Cruelty and Oppression, bringing thither Vices unknown to those former Inhabitants. But what only can follow from this example is, That a People, having a continu'd Succession of Princes, who study to advance the good of the Community, making that the sole Aim of their Government; and directing all their Laws, and Institutions to that End (which was the peculiar felicity of those happy *Americans*) will without other than Natural Light much better practice all social Vertues, than Men set loose from Law and Shame; who tho' Baptiz'd into the Name of Christ have not yet so much as a true Notion of Christianity, to the which, may certainly be added, or than any other People, who tho' they have the Light of the Gospel among them, yet are not govern'd by the Laws thereof; and a truly Christian Common-wealth in this sense, remains yet to be seen in the World; which when it is, the Vertue, and Felicity of such a People will be found much to surpass the (perhaps partial) account which we have of that of the *Peruvians*; whose so long uninterrupted Succession of Excellent Princes, is what only is admirable in the account we have of them; and not the Force of the Light of Nature in those People, who being apparently of tractable, gentle dispositions, and tir'd with the Miseries of a Life to the last degree Brutish, did from the visible wretchedness and inconveniences thereof, gladly obey such whom they believed were (as they told them they were) Divinely sent to teach then a happier way of living. And in the Vertues which these their first Lawgivers taught them, their Successors easily retain'd them; continuing still to maintain in them a perswasion of their Divine Extraction, and Authority. From the which it will be found that this instance of the *Peruvian* Morality makes for the need of Revelation to inforce Natural Religion, and not against it. But how far Revelation is needful to assist Natural Light, will be the best seen in reflecting a little upon what we receive from each of these Guides that God has given us. And if it shall appear from thence that Natural Religion has need of Revelation to support it; and that the Revelation which we have by Jesus Christ is exquisitely adapted to the end of inforcing Natural Religion; this will both be the highest confirmation possible, that to inforce Natural Religion or Morality, was the design of Christianity; and will also shew that to the want of their being in earnest Christians, is to be attributed the immorality of such who, professing Christianity, live immoral Lives. The consequence from whence must be, That to reclaim a Vicious People, it should be consider'd, as the most effectual means of doing so, how to make Men really, and in earnest Christians.

To see what light we receive from Nature to direct our Actions, and how far we are Naturally able to obey that Light; Men must be consider'd purely as in the state of Nature, *viz.* as having no extrinsick Law to direct them, but indu'd only with a faculty of comparing their distant Ideas by intermediate Ones, and Thence of deducing, or infering one thing from another; whereby our Knowledge immediately received from *Sense*, or *Reflection*, is inlarg'd to a view of Truths remote, or future, in an Application of which Faculty of the mind to a consideration of our own Existence and Nature, together with the beauty and order of the Universe, so far as it falls under our view, we may come to the knowledge of a *First Cause*; and that this must be an *Intelligent Being, Wise* and *Powerful*, beyond what we are able to conceive. And as we delight in our selves, and receive pleasure from the objects which surround us, sufficient to indear to us the possession and injoyment of Life, we cannot from thence but infer, that this *Wise* and *Powerful Being* is also most *Good*, since he has made us out of nothing to give us a Being wherein we find such Happiness, as makes us very unwilling to part therewith.

And thus, by a consideration of the Attributes of God, visible in the Works of the Creation, we come to a knowledge of his Existence, who is an Invisible Being: For since *Power, Wisdom* and *Goodness,* which we manifestly discern in the production and conservation of our selves, and the Universe, could not subsist independently on some substance for them to inhere in, we are assur'd that there is a substance where unto they do belong, or of which they are the Attributes.

Which Attributes of God would not be discoverable by us, did we not discern a difference in Things; as between *Power* and *Weakness, Benevolence* and *no Benevolence,* or its contrary; and betwixt directing means to an End, and acting at hap-hazard without any design, or choice: A knowledge, which, by whatever steps convey'd into the mind, is no other than a seeing things to be what they are, and that they cannot but be what they are.

From which diversity and immutability in the Nature of things, there necessarily arises a diversity of respects and relations between them, as unchangeable as the things themselves: wherein the Will of the Creator in reference hereunto is reveal'd to every intelligent Agent, so far as he is made capable of discerning these relations, dependencies and consequences; and whatsoever with respect to his own Actions, such a Being finds resulting from any of these as most conformable to the design of his Creator in making him such a part as he is of the whole, he cannot but consider as the Will of God, thereby dictated to him; since otherwise, God would act contradictiously to his Wisdom in making him what he is.

We being then indu'd, as we are, with a capacity of perceiving and distinguishing these differences of Things; and also with a liberty of acting, or not, suitably and agreeably hereunto; whence we can according to the preference of our own minds, act either in conformity to, or disconformity with, the Will of the Creator (manifested in his Works no less than the Will of any Humane Architect is in his) it follows, That to act answerably to the nature of such Beings as we are, requires that we attentively examine, and consider the several natures of Things, so far as they have any relation to our own actions.

Which attentive consideration of the Works of God objected to our view, implies an exercise thereupon of that Faculty in us by which we deduce, or infer, one thing from another: Whence (as has been said) our knowledge immediately deriv'd to us from sensation, or reflection, is inlarg'd by the perception of remote, or distant Truths. The more obviously eminent advantages accruing to us from which faculty of reason, plainly make known the Superiority of its Nature; and that its suggestions, ought to be hearken'd to by us preferably to those of Sense; where these (as it too often happens) do not concur. For did we know nothing by *Inference* and *Deduction,* both our knowledge and injoyment would be very short of what they now are; many considerable pleasures depending almost intirely upon Reason; and there being none of the greatest Enjoyments of Sense which would not lose their best Relish, separated from those concomitant satisfactions which accompany them only as we are rational Creatures. Neither is it our greatest happiness alone which is manifestly provided for in our being indu'd with this Faculty; but our much greater safety, and preservation likewise; since *these* require a capacity in us of foreseeing distant Events, and directing means to an End, oftentimes through a long train of Actions; which is what we can only do by that in us, whereby the Relations, Dependencies and Consequences of things are discoverable to us.

But as *Reason* is that which either in kind or degree, differences Men from Brutes; and that there are few, if any, who would lose this distinction, it is by common consent acknowledg'd that Reason is in respect of all others, a preferable indowment. And if Beasts, only inferiour to Men in the advantages of this Faculty, appear hereby intended to be subjected to Men, it cannot be less evident That that part in Men which they have in common with Beasts, was likewise design'd by their Maker to be subjected to their Reason also. From All which, it undeniably follows that we do not act answerably to the Will, or pleasure of God, in making us such Creatures as we are, if we either neglect the Search of those Measures of our Actions prescrib'd to us by the discernable Natures of Things; or, if seeing these, we yet conform not our selves thereunto.

Now for any Creature knowingly to oppose the Will of its Creator, is not only disingenuity in regard of what is owing from it to its Sovereign Benefactor, and Folly in respect of that dependence which it has on him for its Being, as it is commonly represented to us to be; but is also in the Nature of Things (simply consider'd) so repugnant to right Reason, that were such a Creature consistent with it self herein, and could act pursuantly to That Will, it would operate to its own destruction; since its Existence evidently depends upon That of its Maker; whose Will, as reveal'd to us, being but a different consideration of his Attributes, the knowledge whereof is all the Knowledge we have of God, cannot be so much as conceiv'd by us separable from the Being of God; unless the God, which we conceive, be a Fiction of our own Imagination, and not the Creator of All Things; who is an invisible Being only knowable to us in, and by, the exemplifications of his Attributes: The infinite Perfection, and the inseparable Correspondence, and Harmony of which (discernable in the Frame and Government of the Universe) plainly tells us, That the Divine Will cannot be (like ours) successive Determinations without dependance, or connection one upon another; much less inconsistent, contradictory, and mutable; but one steady, uniform, unchangeable result of infinite Wisdom and Benevolence, extending to, and including All his Works. So that Sin, or disobedience to our Maker is manifestly the greatest Nonsense, Folly and contradiction conceivable, with regard purely to the immutable perfection of the Divine Nature; and to the Natural constitution of things, independently upon any positive command of God to us, or his irresistible power over us.

But as without a capacity in The Creature to act contrary to the will of the Creator there could be no defect, or self-excellency in any Created Being; contrariety to the Will of God is therefore permitted in the Universe as a necessary result of Creaturely imperfection, under the greatest endowment that a Created Being is capable of having, *viz. That of Freedom or Liberty of Action*: And as the constitution of such Creature, as this, implies that what is *best* in reference to the design of the Creator, and of its own Happiness, should not be always necessarily present to the Mind as

Best; such a Creature may oppose the Will of his Maker with various degrees of Guilt in so doing; or (possibly) with none at all; for no Agent can offend farther than he wilfully abuses the Freedom he has to act.

But God having made Men so as that they find in themselves, very often, a liberty of acting according to the preference of their own Minds, it is incumbent upon them to study the Will of their Maker; in an application of the Faculty of Reason which he has given them, to the consideration of the different respects, consequences, and dependencies of Things, so as to discern from thence, the just measures of their actions in every circumstance and relation they stand plac'd in; which *measures* are nothing else but the dictates resulting from those views which such a consideration of things as this gives us, of what is consonant, or not so, to the design of the Creator in every particular, wherein we are concern'd to act. And these manifestations of his Will, thus discoverable to us, ought to be regarded by us, as his Commands.

Yet however certain it is, that the dictates of *Reason*, or *Nature*, discernable by our natural Faculties, are the commands of God to us, as rational Creatures; it is equally true that the love of happiness (which consists in pleasure) is the earliest, and strongest principle of Humane Nature; and therefore whatever measures Reason does, or might, prescribe, when particular occasions occur, the sentiment of what Men find pleasing or displeasing to them, however contrary to those dictates of right Reason, is very apt to determine their choice. God yet who is the Author of Order, and not of Confusion, has fram'd all things with Consistency, and Harmony; and however, in Fact, it too often happens that we are misled by that strong desire of happiness implanted in us, yet does this no way necessarily interfere with our acting in an intire conformity to the prescriptions of the Law of Reason; but the contrary: For from hence it is that this Law has its Sanction, *viz.* That, duly considering it, we shall evidently find our happiness, and misery, are annex'd to the observance, or neglect, of that unalterable Rule of Rectitude, discoverable to us by the Nature of Things; so that this Rule of Rectitude, or Eternal Will of God, has also the force of a Law given to it by that inseparable accord that there is betwixt our happiness or misery, with our obedience, or disobedience, hereunto. Thus our duty and happiness, can never be divided, but when we prefer a less happiness to a greater; and therein act not conformably to the dictates of our natural desire of happiness, or pleasure; which two Terms differ only in this, that we apply the Term *Pleasure* to any agreeable Sentiment, or Sensation, how small, or short soever in its duration; but that of *Happiness*, only to such degrees of pleasure, as do, in some considerable degree, out-ballance our Evils.

That we are many ways capable of receiving pleasure, we experimentally find; every sense furnishes something to delight, and please us, in its Application to Objects suited to a grateful exercise thereof. And the operations of our own Minds upon the Ideas presented to them by our Senses, afford us also other pleasures, oftentimes preferable by us to those that we receive immediately from Sense. But be our pleasures excited how they will; or whatsoever they consist in, Those that Men receive from the Gratification of antecedent desire, are the pleasures that they have the strongest relish of. *A Good* not desir'd, making (comparatively) but a small Impression upon us.

Now the Gratification of their desires is not always in Men's Power, but oftentimes it is so. It is then often in their choice to procure to themselves pleasure, or not. Whence it is reasonable for them to inquire, since happiness consists in pleasure; and the Gratification of their Desires, and Appetites, always gives them pleasure; whether, or no, to Gratifie *These* should not therefore always be that which should determine their actions in pursuance of this their chief End?

That happiness consisting in pleasure, we are so much the happier as we enjoy more pleasure, must unquestionably, be found true; but that the Gratification of Men's Desires and Appetites cannot therefore be that which should always, as they are rational Agents, determine, or regulate their actions in pursuit of happiness, is no less evident; in that we perceive our selves, and the Things to which we have relation, to be so fram'd, and constituted, in respect one of another, that the Gratification of our present Desires and Appetites, does sometimes for a short, or small pleasure, procure to us a greater, and more durable Pain: and that on the contrary, the denial, or restraint of our present Desires, and Appetites, does sometimes for a short, or small Pain, procure to us a greater, or more durable Pleasure. Since then that we should act contrary to our own end therein, and prefer less pleasure to greater, it is apparent that the Gratification of our present Appetites cannot be that which always, as we are rational Agents, proposing to our selves happiness for our chief end, should determine, or regulate our voluntary actions; present Appetite telling us only what will give us present pleasure; not what will, in the whole, procure to us the most pleasure. What else then appears to be the Rule, or Measure of Men's actions acting purely with respect to the pursuit of happiness as their chief End, but the determinations of that Faculty in them which, in reference to the different properties and relations discernable in Things, can alone be the Judge what will, in the whole, procure to them the most pleasure? And thus the very desire of happiness, or love of pleasure, rightly pursu'd, does oblige us to make the determinations or dictates of Reason, and not the suggestions of present Appetite, the Measure, and Rule of our actions in our pursuit after happiness. Which that we might possess was no doubt the end of our Creator in giving us Being; since he could not stand in need of, or be better'd by our Existence. And if that we might be happy was the end for which God made us, it is most certain that he has neither set any such measures to our Actions, or put any such unhappy Biass upon our Minds, as shall necessarily contradict this his end. Whence it again appears that the love of Pleasure implanted in us (if we faithfully pursue it in prefering always that which will, on the whole, procure to us the most pleasure) can never mislead us from the observance of the Law of Reason: And that this Law enjoyns only a right regulation of our natural desire of pleasure, to the end of our obtaining the greatest happiness that we are capable of: so that there is an inseparable connection, or relation of Moral Good and Evil, with our Natural Good, and Evil. To assert therefore that our chief Good does consist in pleasure, is far from drawing after it any such consequence as many have pretended it does, in prejudice to the Law of Reason, that Natural Revelation of Gods Will to us; since no Man can upon due consideration thereof Judge, That the Gratification of his present Appetites ought to be to him the Measure or Rule of his Actions in consequence of

Pleasures being his chief Good: experience it self, we see, contradicting such a consequence: and that so evidently that I think we do not in fact find that even Those, who the most indulge to their Passions and Appetites, do so as believing upon a cool examination thereof, that to do thus is the truest Wisdom, in consequence of our greatest Good consisting in pleasure; but such Men indulge to their present Appetites meerly as being strongly induc'd (contrary oftentimes to the suggestions of their own minds therein) thro' the love of pleasure, and abhorrence of pain, to do, or forbear whatever they find will procure to them the one, or free them from the other at the present Time; the Gratification whereof They prefer to that which is Future. It is however true that such declamations as are sometimes made against pleasure absolutely (not the irregular pursuit of it) as if pleasure was in its own Nature, a false, and deceitful, not a real and solid Good, have produc'd this ill effect, that many from the absurdity hereof are confirm'd in an evil indulgence of their Appetites, as if to Gratifie These was indeed the truest Wisdom of a rational Creature, in consequence of pleasure, being his chief Good. But they judge not thus from a due examination, or any examination at all of the nature of Things, but from a Reason (if it may be call'd so) of opposition. For so ridiculously weak are a great part of Men in their Reasoning, that seeing they are in the wrong who oppose them, they become from thence as much perswaded, and as well satisfy'd that the contrary to such Mens Assertions is true; or that themselves are in the right, as if they saw that these things really were so. This arguing yet is no more irrational than that whereby a palpable Truth is deny'd, only because some have indeavour'd to draw, or have been thought to have drawn ill consequences from it: Which is yet all the ground of not allowing that Pleasure, and Pain, are truly Good, and Evil; the denying of which, can be of no Service to Morality, but the contrary, since Moral Good, and Evil, consider'd antecedently to any positive Law of our Maker, are apt to be thought but a Notion where that inseparable Relation is overlook'd which there is between actions denominated by us vertuous, or vicious, and the Natural Good, and Evil of Mankind.

Christians, perhaps, need not the confederation of this to inforce their obedience to the Will of their Maker; but as it is a great recommendation of the Precepts of the Gospel to find that they have an exact correspondence with, and conformity to the Nature of Things: So also those who are not influenc'd by, as not being yet thorowly perswaded of this Divine Revelation, will sooner be induced to imbrace Vertue, and contemn the allurements of Vice, when they see These to have the very same reality, in Nature as their Happiness and Misery have; than when (tho' ever so pompously set out) Vertue appears founded only upon nice, or subtle Speculations. But some Men there are so far from approving of any Notion or Theorem being advanc'd with respect to Deists whereby, as such, they may be induc'd to the love of Vertue (which is the best predisposition to the entertainment of Christianity) that they are ready to treat as not being themselves Christians if not as Atheists, any one who in the view of gaining thus much upon these Men assert Vertue by any other Arguments than such as they will not admit of, *viz.* those drawn from Revelation.

However true yet it is that happiness, or our chief Good, does consist in pleasure; it is no less true that the irregular Love of pleasure is a perpetual source to us of Folly, and Misery. That we are liable to the which irregularity, is but a necessary result of our Creaturely imperfection: for we cannot love pleasure, and not love present

26

pleasure: and the love of present pleasure it is which misleads our narrow, and unattentive Minds from a just comparison of the present, with what is future. Nor is it a wonder if we are oftentimes thus mislead; since we frequently wander from the right way with less excuse for doing so: Men, not seldom, going astray from Reason, when the love of present pleasure is so far from misguiding their variously frail Natures, that its allurements will not retain them in the paths of Vertue; and tho' Reason only has Authority to set Bounds to their desires, they subject both Them, and Her to an Unjust and Arbitrary Dominion, equally Foreign to both: A thing manifest, not only in instances here and there, but in the examples of whole Nations; who either by positive institution, or allow'd of Custom, have transgressed against the plainest prescriptions of Reason, in things so far from gratifying their Appetites, as that they are contrary, and even sometimes grievous to Mens natural desires. To account for which, will not here be impertinent; nor (in order to the doing so) to consider first what the Terms *Vertue* and *Religion* have, in their vulgar acceptation, every where generally stood for.

Religion has, I think, been rightly defin'd to be *the knowledge how to please God*, and thus taken, does necessarily include vertue, that is to say, *Moral Rectitude*; but as Men have usually apply'd these Terms *Vertue* and *Religion*, they stand for things very different and distinct, one from another. For by a Vertuous Man, in all Countries of the World, or less Societies of Men, is commonly meant, by those who so call any one, such a Man as steadily adheres to that Rule of his Actions which is establish'd for a Rule in his Country Tribe, or Society, be that what it will. Hence it has been that *Vertue* has in different Times and Places chang'd Face; and sometimes so far, as that what has been esteem'd Vertuous in one Age, and in one Country, has been look'd upon as quite the contrary in others: tho' in all Times and Places, wherein Men have not degenerated into a downright Brutish, or altogether Animal Life (as some whole Nations have done) but have set any Rules, or Measures to their Actions, the dictates of right Reason have more, or less, taken Place with them, so far as the manifest advantages, or rather necessity thereof to the subsistence or convenience of Society, has directed Men. And so much as Custom, or the Injunctions of some Lawgiver inforc'd these dictates of Reason, or Nature, so far and no further, did obedience thereunto denominate Men Vertuous; without any distinction made in reference to these prescriptions, as being Precepts of the Eternal Law of Right, or as obligatory any other ways than as being part of the Law, or Fashion of that Country, or Society, wherein these Rules had prevail'd or were establish'd. A firm and steady adherence to which, whether conformable, or not, to the Law of Reason, being alike that which ever intitled Men to be esteem'd Vertuous among those who profess'd to live by the same Rule.

Now since Man is a Creature that has variable, and disagreeing Inclinations, as having passions very changeable, and oftentimes contradictory one to another, there is not any fix'd Rule, or Measure, whatsoever that can possibly be set to his Actions, which can constantly be adher'd to by him, without some difficulty, or uneasiness; because any steady, and unalterable Rule must necessarily oftentimes, thwart and cross his changeable Appetites, and differing Inclinations; even altho' that Rule was contriv'd, and intended ever so much, to be indulgent to the Passions, and Desires of Humane Nature in general.

Conformity therefore of Mens actions to any fix'd, and unvariable Rule, is a thing of some difficulty, be the Rule what it will: And therefore Transgression against that Rule which Men profess'd themselves oblig'd to act by, has always, every where been; and but few Men comparatively, were strictly Vertuous: That is, did in all things conform, or sincerely endeavour to conform their Actions to that, which they acknowledged for the Rule of them.

Those yet who believ'd a Superior Invisible Power that made them, could not be satisfy'd with themselves in Transgressing against that which they thought ought to be their Rule: For however they understood this Rule to be deriv'd, they yet believ'd it carry'd with it, some way or other, an obligation upon them to Obedience; since otherwise they would not have look'd upon it as a Rule. Now, as they could not know that God would not punish their Disobedience to That which they look'd upon as obliging them to Obedience; but, on the contrary, had more, or less, Reason to apprehend that he would do so, They therefore (thinking him to be an exorable as well as an Omniscient, and Omnipotent Being) were hereby on These occasions taught to deprecate his Vengeance, and implore his Mercy: And hence the more Guilty and Fearful came to invent Attonements, Expiations, Penances and Purgations, with all that various Train of Ceremonies which attended those Things; Naturally imagining that the Divine Nature resembled their own; and thence believing that they should the more easily appease his Anger, and avert the effects of his Wrath, if by such means, as these, they did, as it were, in Gods behalf Revenge upon themselves their Disobedience to him. And as the Solemnity of these Matters requir'd peculiar Hands to Execute them; and Devotion exacted that such should be liberally rewarded, and highly respected for their Pious performances; from hence the profit which some reap'd by these things, as well as the satisfaction that others found therein, who were unwilling to be rigorously restrain'd by the Rule of their Actions, yet were uneasie under the reproaches of their Consciences when they transgressed against it, made these Inventions, and the value set upon them, to be daily improv'd; till Men at last have sought to be, and have effectually been perswaded that they might render themselves acceptable to God without indeavouring sincerely to obey the Rule by which they profess'd to believe they were oblig'd to live; and that even when they did think that this was a Law giv'n them by God himself.

Now the great practicers, and promoters of the abovesaid things, are every where Those who are generally esteem'd, and call'd *Religious*. Whence the Term *Religion* appears ordinarily to have stood for nothing else, but *some Expedient, or other, found out to satisfy Men that God was satisfied with them, notwithstanding that their Consciences reproach'd them with want of Conformity to the acknowledg'd Rule, or Law of their Actions.*

Having premis'd thus much concerning the Notions Men vulgarly have had of *Vertue* and *Religion,* let us now proceed to see how it has come to pass, That they have with Allowance, Approbation, and oftentimes, with injunction of their Lawmakers and Governours, transgress'd against the most visible Dictates of the Law of Nature, or Reason, in Things not favourable to their Natural Passions and

Appetites; but even, sometimes, contrary thereunto; as are denying themselves the lawfullest Enjoyments of Life; Macerating their Bodies; Prostituting their Wives; and exposing their Off-spring and Themselves to cruel Torments, and even Death it self. The cause of which I think appears plainly to be; that Mankind having been generally convinc'd that there was a Maker of themselves and of the World, who they concluded was as well able to take cognisance of what they did, as to produce them into Being; and to whom they could not believe that all the Actions of his Creatures were alike pleasing, or displeasing; they became fearful (as has been said) of incurring his displeasure, whenever they did any thing which their Consciences reproach'd them for: From the which Fear of a Superior invisible Power, inspecting their Actions, they were early induc'd to hearken to, and follow such who profess'd themselves to have some Knowledge Supernaturally reveal'd to them of God's Will. And we find, in the Histories of all Nations, that the generality of Mankind were perswaded (contrary to the Sentiments of some Modern Deists) That it was a thing very congruous to the Divine Being, that he should in this way reveal to Men his pleasure concerning them; since the greatest part, every where, did with little difficulty give Credit to such who had the confidence to affirm to them, that they were sent by God to teach them what he required of them: the which being so, a submission of Mens Reason to the dictates of suppos'd inspir'd Teachers must necessarily follow: and they from thence become liable to be impos'd upon, all the ways that could serve the ends of such who made use of this pretence to promote thereby any Interest of their own, or others.

And as there is scarce any Country can be nam'd where there has not been these pretences to Revelation; so no Instance, I believe, can be found of any Institution or generally approv'd of Practice, opposite to the obvious Dictates of Nature, or Reason, and not in Favour of Mens Appetites, which does not appear, or on good ground may not be presumed to have been receiv'd on this pretence of Supernatural Revelation; which has ever procur'd the firmest adherence to any New Institution whatsoever; and was very sufficient to make the absurdest things be swallow'd equally with the most reasonable; it being undeniably true, that whatever God does Command, his Creatures are under an equal Obligation of Obedience thereunto.

Some Men, it is likely, there have, in all Ages and Places, been, who were too Sagacious to admit of that as Revelation from God, which manifestly oppos'd Natural Light; and who needed a proof of the Divine Mission of such pretenders as these. But the unthinking Multitude were ever Credulous; and thence have been always practic'd upon in various kinds, and measures, as has best suited the occasion: Those who have had vicious Inclinations, or little Aims, and short views, having impos'd upon them suitably to their Ends: And such as have had larger comprehensions, generous designs, and Minds above Vulgar, Base and Sordid Passions, having answerably to their Aims, serv'd themselves of the same credulity. Of the last kind were such who have propos'd the reclaiming of Men from vices more obviously prejudicial to Society, and civil Government; thereby to erect or restore some flourishing Kingdom, or common-wealth; And these, tho' they have deceived Men, in making them believe that their Laws were Divinely inspir'd, have yet deservedly been Honour'd by them as Benefactors, because of that happiness which they procur'd to them thereby, in this World; beyond which, their views extended not, as having no knowledge of a future Life. The which sort of Men, however rational, and Vertuous they were, yet (like other pretenders to Revelation) that they might the better procure Authority to their Dictates, did with their civil Institutions, mix Holy Mysteries; and that usually as peculiar Secrets taught them by some Divinity. They also, how much soever they, perhaps, secretly contemn'd such things, did yet generally pay a great outward regard to matters of Religion; which have ever abounded in the best Govern'd, and most Flourishing Kingdoms, and Common-wealths.

Now (as has been already said) the exact observers of the civil Institutions of their Country, or Customs of their Ancestors, were look'd upon as Men of Vertue; and whoso apply'd himself eminently to the observation of such superstitions as consisted of Sacrifices, Processions, Lustrations, &c. with a various Train of Pompous Ceremonies, diversify'd according to the Phancies of their Authors, was look'd upon as a Religious Man; whilst there was a third sort of Men (inconsiderable always in their Number) who judged, by the true rule of Reason, what was right, and what was wrong, in the first of these; and who contemning the Fopperies of the last, were oftentimes (thro' their means who most found their Account in those Matters) in danger of passing with the silly People for Atheists: such as search for their opinions, and the Measures of their Actions in the Reason and Truth of Things, having always been very unacceptable to Those whose Interest it has been to keep up the Credit and Authority of vain Traditions and Superstitious Practices; because if *These* should be hearken'd to, *Those* Apprehended that they should become useless.

Men of this third sort are They who are vertuous in a Rational and Christian estimation; for if adherence to the Rule of Mens Actions (be that what it will) denominates Men vertuous among those of their own perswasion therein; then That which denominates a Man vertuous amongst Those who take the prescriptions of right Reason, or of the Gospel (for these are but one, and the same, differently promulg'd) for the Rule of their Actions, must be an adherence to the Law of right Reason, or of this Revelation: Which Rule, is not (as all others are) a changeable, because (as we have seen) no Arbitrary thing; it being founded in Relations, and Connexions, which are as immutable as that determinate constitution in Things, which makes every thing what it is. From whence it has been that such Men in all Ages, and Places, as were above the prejudices of their Country Religion, and Manners, *viz.* such as we have now spoken of, have ever had much the same Sentiments in respect of Vertue. But these have always been but a small Number: Custom, and blind Opinion, have ever govern'd the World; and the light of Reason has neither appear'd to Men to be, nor in Fact been any where sufficient to direct the generality of Mankind to Truth; as some imagine it capable of doing; who because of that clear Evidence which Reason gives to those verities that Revelation has already taught them, think that they owe, or might have ow'd to this light of Reason what they are not indebted to it for; and what it is a Thousand to One odds they would not have receiv'd from it, had they been Born where there was no other than Natural Light.

For we find not any Country in any Age of the World, wherein Men did generally acknowledge, by the meer force of Reason, Natural Religion in its full extent; or where the Law of Nature was by the Light of Nature universally own'd. Some Dictates of it as suggested by necessity, or convenience, having only been receiv'd, (as has been already said) but not distinguish'd from the most Arbitrary Institutions of Men; altho' it is probable that the greater Conformity any Law had to the dictates of right Reason, it did the more universally and easily obtain Belief of its being divinely reveal'd to him who pretended so to have receiv'd it; and this apparently it was which gave so great Success to the *Peruvian* Lawgivers; whose Idolatry was the most specious that was possible; and whose Rules of Living (pretended to have been receiv'd by them from the Sun, their Father, and Vicegerent of *Pachacama*, the Supream Invisible and Unapproachable God) were highly suitable to the dictates of right Reason.

This Law nevertheless not being receiv'd by that People but as a Supernatural Revelation, the great Morality of the *Peruvians* affords no Argument against, but (on the contrary) proves strongly the need of Revelation; since whatever Force of Reason these Natural Truths did appear to this People to carry with them, when represented as divine Commands, this light had never yet attracted their sight purely by its own Brightness; nor ever has any where done so, but here and there in a few Instances of Persons of more than ordinarily inquisitive Minds; and (probably) for the most part, exempted by a happy priviledge of Nature from the servitude of sensual, and sordid Passions.

And tho' nothing can be more evident to those who reflect thereupon, than that Mens Actions should be regulated, and directed by that Faculty in them which shows them the different properties, relations, and dependencies of things, and not by their Appetite, which only can tell what will at the present please, or offend them; not what will, upon the whole, procure to them the most pleasure, or uneasiness; yet such appears to be the unreflecting Nature of the generality of Mankind, and such their fondness of present pleasure, as either not to consider this Truth, or when they do so, to be induc'd (in consequence thereof) to obey the most manifest dictates of Reason, or Natural Light, which will lay any restraint upon their pleasing, and, oftentimes, violent Inclinations: Much less will they be at pains to search for any such Measures of their Actions in the Constitution and dependances of things; which is indeed what the far greater part of Men have not the Capacity, or Leisure to do: Neither are Any able to do this so early as to prevent their irregular Inclinations from being first strengthen'd and confirm'd by ill habits: which when once they are, Reason does in vain oppose them, how clear soever her dictates appear. On the contrary, our Passions grown strong, do usually so far corrupt our Reason as to make her joyn parties with them against her self; we not only doing amiss, but likewise finding Arguments to justify our so doing, even to our selves as well as others.

But there is still, beyond this, a farther impediment to Mens obeying the Law of Nature, by vertue of the meer Light of Nature; which is, that they cannot, in all circumstances, without Revelation, make always a just estimate in reference to their happiness. For, tho' it is demonstrable that the Law of Reason is the Law of God,

31

yet the want of an explicite knowledge of the penalty incur'd by the breach of that Law, makes it not to be evident to all Men that the incuring of this penalty shall (in all cases) make the preference of breaking this Law, an ill Bargain: which it may, sometimes not be to many, in regard of the discernable natural consequences of such a Transgression. For tho' observance of the Law of Reason is, in the constitution of Natural Causes, visibly to those who consider it (generally speaking) the means of our greatest happiness, even in this present World, yet if there be no future Life (which that there is, is made certain to us, only by the Revelation thereof in the Gospel) to answer in for Transgression of this Law; the breach of it may, tho' not naturally, yet accidentally, in some cases, conduce to Mens greater happiness; and, very often, notwithstanding that to have obey'd the Law of Reason they may discern would have been better for them than to have follow'd their Appetites, had they been early so accustom'd, yet now that they have contracted different Habits, which are like a *Right Hand*, or *Eye* to them, the difficulty of a new course of Life may appear too great for the attempt of it to be adviseable; since the consideration of the shortness and uncertainty of Life may make Men apt to say to themselves on such occasions,

Who would lose the present Hour, For one that is not in his Power? Or not be happy now he may, But for a Future Blessing stay: Who know not he shall live a Day?

The Revelation of an Eternal Life after this, with an express Declaration of Everlasting Rewards and Punishments annex'd to our Obedience, or Disobedience, to the Law of Nature (tho' such a Future State may be reasonably infer'd from all things happening alike to the Good, and to the Bad in this World, and from Men's Natural desire of Immortality) is yet but a necessary inforcement of the Law of Nature to the far greatest part of Mankind, who stand in need of this knowledge, and are uncapable of an Inference so repugnant to what their Senses daily tell them in the case; and wherein the Truth asserted has scarcely ever procur'd an unwavering assent from the most rational of the Heathen Philosophers themselves. Now the unquestionable certainty of a Future State, wherein Men shall receive Everlasting Rewards, and Punishments, we alone owe the knowledge of to Jesus Christ, *who only has brought Life and Immortality to Light.* The willingest to believe the Souls Immortality were before our Saviours coming, at best, doubtful concerning it; and the generality of Mankind, were yet far less perswaded of it.

Fables indeed concerning a life hereafter (wherein there were Rewards and Punishments) the *Greeks* had; and from them, they were deriv'd to some other Nations; but that for Fables they were taken is evident, and we are expressly told so by *Diodorus Siculus*, who applauding the Honours done to Good Men at their Funerals, by the *Egyptians, because of that warning and encouragement which it gave to the Living to be mindful of their Duty,* says, *That the Greeks, as to what concern'd the Rewards of the Just, and the Punishment of the Impious, had nothing among them but invented Fables and Poetical Fictions which never wrought upon Men for the Amendment of their Lives; but on the contrary, were despis'd and laugh'd at by them.*

Whether, or no, Men should subsist after Death depending plainly upon the good Pleasure of their Maker, the Pagan World (to whom God had not reveal'd his Will herein) could not possibly have any certainty of a Life after this. Arguments there were (as has been said) that might induce rational Men to hope for a future Existence as a thing probable; and they did so: But the Gross of Mankind saw not the Force of these Reasonings to be perswaded thereby of a thing so inconceivable by them as that the Life of the Person was not totally extinguish'd in the Death of the Body; and a Resurrection to Life, was what they thought not of, the certainty of which, together with future Reward and Punishment, by enabling us to make a right estimate concerning what will most conduce to our happiness, plainly brings this great encouragement to our Observance of the Law of God, that it lets us see our happiness, and our Duty, are inseparably united therein; since whatever pleasure we voluntarily deprive our selves of in this World from preference of Obedience to God's Commands, it shall be recompenced to us manifold in the World that is to come: So that now we can find our selves in no Circumstance, wherein our Natural Desires of Happiness, or love of Pleasure, can rationally induce us to depart from the Rule of our Duty.

The little which has been said, do, methinks, sufficiently evince the need of Revelation both to Teach and inforce Natural Religion: But the defectiveness of the Light of Nature to this end, is a Verity of so great use to be establish'd, that the consideration thereof should not be left upon such short Reflections as these; was not this Truth at large made out in a late Treatise intitled, *The reasonableness of Christianity as delivered in the Scriptures*.

A work which the unhappy mistakes and disputes among us concerning the Christian Religion, makes useful to all Men; and which has been peculiarly so to many, as the only Book wherein they have found the insufficiency of Natural Light to Natural Religion, has been fully shewed, although that to reconcile Men to, or establish them in the belief of Divine Revelation, nothing was more requisite to make this appear, in an Age wherein the prevalency of Deism has been so much and so justly complain'd of.

But against the insufficiency of Natural Light to the ends of Natural Religion, the World having been so many Ages without it, is, by some, thought an Objection: For, if Supernatural Light had been so needful as is pretended to be, how could it comport, say they, with the Wisdom of God not to have given it to Men sooner and more universally?

To judge of all the Ends and Designs of the Divine Wisdom in the Creation or Government of the World, is to suppose that we have a comprehension of God's Works, adequate or commensurate thereunto; which is not only to conceive of his Wisdom as not being infinite, but even to circumscribe it within very narrow bounds. If the Wisdom of God, (like his other Attributes) does infinitely surpass our reach, his Views must, for that reason, be necessarily oftentimes, as much beyond our short Sight. For us then, when we see not the reason why any thing is, to take upon us to say that such a thing does, or does not comport with the Wisdom of God, must needs be the highest Folly that can be, since it implies a presumption, that we see all in respect of such a Subject that God sees: And the Objection here made turns only upon the *unaccountableness* of the Divine Wisdom herein to our Understandings. For God's dealing thus with Men, can by no means be said by us to imply any *contradiction* to his Wisdom. Whilst we having an assurance highly Rational (from those numberless Worlds which surround us) that we are but a small part of the Intellectual Creation of our Maker; and being certain that our abode here bears but a very inconsiderable proportion of Time to millions of Ages, and is as nothing to Eternity, cannot tell but that to know much more than we do, in this State, of the intire Scheme of Providence with respect to the whole extent of intelligent Beings, may be necessary to our seeing the Beauty of anyone part of the design of our Creator. And it is the most suitable to the All-comprehensive Wisdom of God for us to conceive, that without having this knowledge, we may be far less able to judge of the Divine oeconomy, in reference to his Dealings with us here, than he who should see but one Scene of a Dramma, would thereby be capacitated to judge of the Plot or Design of the whole. In Objecting therefore against the need of Revelation to support Natural Religion, because that we understand not why, if Revelation was necessary to this end, the World had it no sooner: Men are guilty of so great an Absurdity as to argue from a Matter only unknown to them against the reality of that evidently *is*: Which is always irrational to do; but is especially so, when, if we cannot answer what is Objected, we yet see plainly that That Objection may be very answerable, and accountable for, even to our Conceptions; were but our views a little more enlarged, and such as, perhaps, they shall be hereafter.

But in urging this consideration as sufficient to silence any Objection to the needfulness of Revelation from its lateness and want of Universality; I suppose not that the Divine, oeconomy is herein actually incomprehensible by Men; or at least, may not be accounted for, if not demonstratively aright, yet suitably to the Divine Attributes: and a due reflection upon the intire design of Christianity, so far as it is reveal'd to us, will, it is likely, conduct us best to a sight hereof. But our present business is not this inquiry, but to see what those advantages are which we receive by the Revelation of Jesus Christ, the design of whole coming into the World appears to have been, to inforce the Rule of Rectitude, by setting it in a clearer Light, with the manifest Attestation of Divine Authority, and promulging it as the Law of God, by Declaration of eternal Rewards and Punishments, annexed to the observance or breach thereof.

Yet to deliver clearer and more excellent Precepts of Morality; to attest to the Divinity hereof by Miracles; or to bring Immortalitie to light, were not (as the means of inforcing Natural Religion) the whole business for which Christ took our Nature upon him. It was a Decree as immutable as the Divine Nature, that no unrighteous thing should have everlasting Life: Wherefore all, both Jews and Gentiles having broken the Law, and being thereby condemn'd (since the Law necessarily requir'd perfect Righteousness, and could admit of no abatement thereof) Christ came to establish betwixt God and Man, a Covenant of Grace in order to Mens obtaining eternal Life, which they could not obtain by the Works of the Law. The which Covenant of Grace was, that to as many as believe in his Son, taking him for their King, and submitting to his Law, God would grant remission of their Sins; and that

34

this *their Faith should be imputed to them for Righteousness*; that is, accepted of by him, in lieu of perfect Obedience, in all such who sincerely indeavour'd to live up to the Precepts of Christ, their Lord.

Men have ever been solicitous, to reconcile Pardon of Sin to the Purity of God's Nature, which has expos'd them (as we have seen) to divers Delusions, and to wearisome and costly Superstitions; even sometimes to the giving *the Fruit of their Bodies to attone for the sins of their Souls*. All the Forms of Pagan Religion have abounded with Institutions of this Nature; and that of the Jews consisted very much of tiresome and unpleasant performances; which being Types and Shadows of him that was to come, were practis'd to the same purpose. All which things we are freed from by the Gospel; *Christ having offer'd up himself once for all, through whom forgiveness of Sin is preached to as many as believe in him*, truly repenting of their past Sins, and *walking in newness of Life*, conformably to the Law of him their Master; but and if, thro' humane Weakness or Imbecillity, we do Sin, he is our *Advocate with the Father*, who for the sake of him his Beloved Son, will justify, or accept as Righteous, those who truly believe in him, whence we are justify'd by God's free Grace or Favour, and not by the Works of the Law, against which all have transgressed, and fail'd of a perfect Obedience.

The great end then of Christianity is (in short) to teach us effactually to *renounce all Ungodliness and every evil work*, by declaring to us, that if we sincerely repent of our Sins past, and indeavour, for the time to come, to obey the Law of our Lord and Master Jesus Christ, which is no other than the Law of Reason, or the eternal Rule of Right, we need not despair of God's Mercy from the Imperfection of our Obedience; since he will for the sake of his Son, pardon their Sins who believe in him: Sincere indeavours after perfect Righteousness being accepted in those who believe in Christ as if they attained it, which is call'd, *the Righteousness of Faith*. And thus our Blessed Lord, that he might *purchase to himself a peculiar people zealous of good Works*, has propos'd to his Followers the strongest Motives and Encouragements that are conceivable to induce free Agents to Obedience, putting them at once upon using their utmost Diligence to *fullfil the Law*; yet, at the same time, delivering them from the fear that their defective *Righteousness should* render their Labour vain in the Lord, by assuring them that he will be merciful to their Sins.

The which Christian Doctrine concerning the forgiveness of Sins (contrary to that of other Religions) effectually obliges Men to use their utmost care not to commit Sin, and leaves no room for the Lusts of their Hearts, or devices of cunning Men to deceive them by any Superstitious Inventions of expiating or attoning for Transgression; whereby Vertue (as we have seen) was always undermin'd. For, tho' in the Christian Religion, there is an abatement of the rigour and severity of the Law, which could not but require an unsinning Obedience; yet we are therein taught, that Jesus Christ is the only Attonement for Sin: And such a Faith in him as makes us to become his obedient Subjects, is the only means to us of Salvation: An inforcement of the Law of Righteousness which was wanting to the Pagan World; whose persuasion of the placability of the Divine Nature (as we have seen) generally taught them, only to find out such imaginary ways of appeasing God's Anger, and expiating for their Sins, as did more or less supersede their indeavours after Obedience to the Law.

Whence it appears that the assurance of future Existence, with the knowledge of eternal Rewards and Punishments annex'd to Mens Observance, or not observance of the Law of Reason had Men had it, without the Revelation of the Gospel, would not have been so universal or powerful an inforcement of Obedience to them as it is to us; to whom together with this, is preach'd also the Doctrine of forgiveness of Sins, through Faith in Jesus Christ. For the consciousness of transgression against this Law, which, under such a Penalty exacted their Obedience, must either have driven Men into despair of being accepted by God, whence they would have given over the indeavours of obeying him as a fruitless Labour; or else if they believ'd that God would accept of some Compensation for their defective Righteousness, they would have been induc'd no less, but even more strongly from their knowledge of a future Life, than they were without it, to seek to attone the Divine Wrath by such ways as would inevitably draw on a neglect of conformity to his Law. Whereas Christianity doth provide against both these Mistakes, in that it assures us that God will accept of our imperfect Obedience for the sake of his Son, if we believe in him, and withal sincerely indeavour to obey him; whereby Faith does plainly *not make void, but establish the Law*, it laying the highest Obligation as well as Encouragement that is possible upon Men to do their utmost to live up to the Prescriptions of it.

And thus the Christian Religion, we find, is every way admirably adapted by the Divine Wisdom, to the end of inforcing the eternal Law of Reason or Nature; which evidently needed this inforcement. From whence it is manifest, that whoso directly or indirectly teaches Men to look upon Christianity as separable from Morality, does the most that is possible misrepresent it; and therein (as effectually as they can do so) undermine both Natural and Reveal'd Religion; the latter of which dispences not with any breach of the former; and exempts us only from the burthen of such outward performances as have no Efficacy to the making Men better, but often do make them very much worse; they conceiving that they are able, thereby, to expiate or attone for their Sins; whence they become less careful in regard of their Duty: A Natural effect of all those things, beneficial alone to the contrivers or directors of them; who, by means thereof, have liv'd in Ease and Plenty upon other Peoples Labours, whilst they (instead of repining thereat) were skilfully taught to reverence them for their usefulness.

Such Men as these profited not a little by the superstition of the People; and therefore could not but always have an interest opposite to that of Vertue: Since the more vertuous Men were, the less they stood in need of, or minded those Matters, of which these managers of Mysteries and Ceremonies had the gainful direction. No wonder then at all was it that the Gospel found so much opposition, whose design was so Diametrically contrary to the interest of a Party every where in such Power and Credit; and whose Author so expresly declared, that his coming was to abolish all such Institutions and Practices.

The Power of God yet prevail'd in spight of that of Men; and Christianity in a little time had spread itself through the Roman Empire.

What remedy then remain'd more fit to be devis'd by the Devil or evil Men, to make the Gospel of no effect, than under specious pretences of owning and honouring it, to corrupt it with the old Pagan Principles and Practices, introduc'd under a Christian Disguise? But it being so plainly deliver'd in the whole Tenour of the New Testament, that *Christ being once for all offer'd up, there remained no more Sacrifice for Sin*; and that he came to teach Men *to worship God in Spirit and, in Truth*. There was no room left for the searchers for their Religion in these Holy Oracles to be led into the formerly mention'd Pagan Superstitions. The Scriptures therefore must be discarded, or, what was the same thing, shut up from vulgar Readers: Which were all but those who had made it their interest to mislead others by their Explications: The which, together with vain Traditions, supported by the Authority of reverend Names, coming in the place of Scripture, were enjoyn'd to be receiv'd equally with Divine Truths on Terrour of eternal Punishment to as many as could be so persuaded, but to be sure of Temporal Penalty to all who durst withstand this violence done to the common reason of Mankind.

The which Spirit of Imposition and Persecution began to shew itself very early among the Professors of Christianity: And so soon as these were arm'd with secular Power, they fail'd not to make use of it one against another, for imposing of Humane Inventions to the neglect of what all profess'd to believe God indispensibly requir'd of them. The which *Mystery of Iniquity*, tho' it *already worked*, in the Apostles Days, yet could not be reveal'd even 'till the power of Heathen *Rome* was taken out of the way: And Christianity had Civil as well as Ecclesiastical Jurisdiction, by their Religions, becoming that of the Empire: Which, when it did, Antichrist soon appear'd in his full Dimensions; and the Christian World became a very Aceldama; A History of which (sad as it is) might perhaps, with some pleasure, be perus'd, were those Tragedies now at an end; or the Reformed part of Christendom had no share in the Guilt.

We generally indeed exclaim against the Cruelties of the *Roman* Church exercis'd over Men, on account or pretence of Religion: And it is true, that they have excell'd herein; yet all Parties among us, proportionally to the extent of their Power, have practis'd the same thing; and the *Best*, when restrain'd from it by the Civil Magistrate, make it evidently appear, that they bear that restraint uneasily.

But whilst the first Spring, which moves such *Animosities* is a desire in *ambitious* and *ill* Men or *Dominion*; well-meaning ignorant People are misled by these from the Truth of the Gospel, to such Zeal for some distinguishing Tenets or Forms as if the stress of Christianity lay in those things: And that our Religion consisted not in such a Faith in Jesus Christ, as to receive him for our King, becoming his obedient Subjects; but in the belief of Opinions, which have no influence upon our Practice, to the making us live more vertuously; or in Worshipping God after some peculiar Mode or Fashion. And thus among us Christians, as heretofore in the Heathen

World, *Vertue* and *Religion* are again distinguish'd; and Religion as something more excellent (and, to be sure, more easy) does still, as formerly it did, eat out Vertue.

Among our selves it is true, that those of the Establish'd Church do generally dislike a distinction often made by some others of a *Moral* and a *Religious* Man; Nor, usually, are our Divines wanting to represent from the Pulpit the necessity there is of a good Life to render Men acceptable to God. But many who condemn such a Doctrine as separates Religion from Morality, do yet in their practices make the like distinction, which may well be presum'd to have been one great cause of their having preach'd up Vertue so ineffectually as they have done. That which People *say* having ordinarily less influence upon others, than what they see them *Do*. And in regard of our earliest Apprehensions concerning Vertue and Religion, it is certain that these are form'd in Children much more from what they observe in the Conversations or Actions of such Persons as they esteem, than by set Discourses that they now and then hear from the Pulpit; which they can neither understand nor attend to early enough to receive from those Principles that shall influence them. But so soon (at the least) as they are capable of minding and understanding Sermons, they (where the thing is remarkable by others) do also take notice of it, if he who frequently recommends a good Life to them, does not in his own Conversation, and in the respect he expresses for Vertue in the Persons of others, shew that he indeed prefers it answerably to the Praises he gives it. And if such a Preacher, as this, shall openly live in the practice of any known Immorality; or not doing so himself shall yet manifestly prefer in his esteem those who do so, is it not natural, for them who look upon this Man as a guide to Heaven, to conclude from hence, that in reference to the obtaining of Eternal Happiness, Vertue is not the thing, the most essentially requisite; and much less certainly will they think it to be so with respect to this present World, if they find their pious Instructor not only to choose the Society of Persons Profligate and Debauch'd for his Friends and Companions; but also (on all occasions) to labour the promotion of the like Men to Employments of the highest Truth, in preference of others of acknowledg'd Integrity and Sobriety of Life: The avow'd Reason whereof being only that the first of these are by the Doctor held the more Orthodox in Religion; is it not unavoidable, even to a Child, to conclude, that Vertue is not the best recommendation in his Opinion, whatever he sometimes seems to assert, when he is shewing his Rhetorick in the Pulpit. And since he is an Authoriz'd Teacher of Religion, will not (so far as his example influences) Vertue and Religion be probably consider'd as distinct things, the latter of which, as it always has had, always will have the preference.

The same Consequence with this must needs, in like manner, follow, where Parents (whose Practices have usually the greatest Authority with their Children) do in this manner express their uncharitable Zeal for their Opinions, by them call'd Orthodoxy: And such, no less effectually, teach the separating of Religion from Vertue, than those whom they, perhaps, greatly condemn for making this distinction in Terms; tho' it is true, that That sort of Men who do use this distinction in their Discourses, do seldom fail of practising accordingly: None having usually a more fiery Zeal than such People have for their Orthodox, or, what is call'd by them, sound Doctrine; and the only difference is, that these Men are herein more consistent with themselves than the former, since their Words and their Actions correspond.

38

Nor less consentaneous to their Opinions are they, in not taking much Pains to inculcate into their Children (as they not often do) the Principles and early Habits of Vertue: For if Vertue, or Morality is so far from being any way that which shall intitle Men to Salvation, that it is not so much as a means, or good predisposition to what shall do so, (God oftentimes to shew his Free Grace preferring the greatest Persons to the most Moral Reasons) which is what these Peoples Teachers frequently tell them; as there appears indeed but little Reason why they should be vertuous, so there cannot be any more why they should indeavour to make others so. Those of these Sentiments are yet generally (tho' not methinks alike conformable to their Doctrines) very Solicitous for what they call *Religious Education*. But how little this will supply the defect of early Principles, and Habits of Vertue, will be visible when we reflect upon what that, which they esteem to be Religious Education does consist in; for commonly it is only in Teaching Children some Form of sound Words as they conceive them to be; in the greatest part, unintelligible to their Learners, or uninstructive of their Ignorance; and in accustoming them to hear many Sermons; which do as little inform them; and wherein Morality is too often represented as, no ways, available to Salvation: and, what is still worse, even (sometimes) as that which shall rank Men among the hateful to, and accursed of God.

The reading of the Bible is, I presume (at the least) as much practic'd by those as by the generality of any other Perswasion; but they study no more than others do to understand it; and (on the contrary) are rather with greater tenaciousness so possess'd by the Sentiments and Opinions of their Teachers, as to be almost uncapable of consulting the word of God without prejudice; or observing any thing therein that is contrary to the Doctrines of their Sect: that *Analogy of Faith* by which they are sure the Scriptures ought always to be interpreted; the obscurest parts whereof their Teachers insist the most upon; whence the Ignorantest Persons of these as well as the more knowing, are usually far less conversant in the plain Doctrines of Jesus Christ, than in St. *Pauls* difficult Epistles; which, as heretofore, *many who are unlearn'd wrest to their own Destruction*, tho' their needs, I think, no skill but that of Attention to what the Apostle is speaking of, to see that he teaches none of those Doctrines which many are taught to believe he delivers to the prejudice of Morality, or good Works; but quite the contrary.

Now what help can such Instruction as this give to the subduing the corrupt Affections, and the bridling betimes the inordinate Desires and Appetites of Humane Nature, whereby Men are inabled to live like rational Creatures, and to acquit themselves well in all the Relations they shall be hereafter plac'd in, in the World? When it does not so much as perswade them, or even allow them to think that these are the things by which they shall be judg'd at the Last Day; but substitutes in the place hereof groundless Conceits, and a presumptious, Faith, which so far teaches them to neglect Obedience as that if they pursu'd the just consequence of their own Doctrine (a thing few People do) they would have no Morality at all: And how rarely soever these consequences are follow'd so far as they would lead Men, yet that they are too much so, is visible in that little concern which such People take (as has been now observ'd) in training up their Children betimes in the knowledge and practice of Vertue; so necessary to the making them hereafter Vertuous, that rarely are any found eminently to be so, where this means has been neglected; even many who are always very sincere in the Profession of Religion, having (thro' the want of this early care taken of them) their Passions never subjected to their Reason; which renders them all their Lives long uneasie to themselves, and others: Whereby also the very profession of Religion is dishonour'd, and evil spoken of.

In the Church of *England*, (whatever her Articles may be thought to teach) there are not many now who hold these Opinions; and such as do not so, rightly looking upon Vertue as the great perfection of Humane Nature, and the End which Christianity is intended to promote, do accordingly (if they are serious in their Religion) instruct their Children much better than those abovementioned are wont to do theirs; at least, they design it: For it is true that the performance does often fall short; because (as has been said) their Actions correspond not with their Instructions; and also from hence That Zeal for Morality makes some, in recommending thereof, too forgetful of that Doctrine of Faith, without which, as works avail not, so also the greatest encouragement to, and inforcement of Morality, is lost. And when any who are profess'd Teachers of the Christian Religion do this, such Men do frequently confirm in their wrong Apprehensions concerning it, those whom they would convince of mistaking the design of the Gospel; since *Faith* is so evidently therein the Doctrine of Salvation, that They who never preach it, are not altogether without Reason suspected either of not understanding Consequences, or else of not being in earnest Christians, but conceal'd Deists, and Betrayers of the Christian Religion. Altho' the Truth herein for the most part is, that one Error unhappily produces another, and the partial regard of some to the Doctrine of Faith (which yet they misrepresent) as if the whole business of our Salvation consisted in That, has been an occasion to other Men of as partially espousing the Doctrine of Good Works; whilst in their heat against what is contrary to Truth in respect thereof, they establish not sufficiently that Justifying Faith of the Gospel, by which alone Men shall obtain Eternal Life, and not by their Works: the best Men's Obedience having (as has been already observ'd) imperfection in it; from whence all are necessarily condemn'd by the Rigour of the Law, and must accordingly be found Guilty, by him, *Who is of Purer Eyes than to behold Iniquity*; had not God, in Mercy to Mankind, been pleas'd to establish *a New Covenant of Grace* in compliance with the Terms whereof, *viz.* Faith in his Son, they may obtain Eternal Life. A Doctrine (as has been seen) the most highly conducing that is possible to the making Men labour after the perfectest Obedience. The Exalters of *Faith* therefore in opposition to *Good Works* do not more undermine *Morality,* than the Advancers of the Doctrine of *Good Works* to the Exclusion of *Free Grace,* do undermine Reveal'd, and in consequence thereof, Natural Religion also. The which two sort of Men divide, if one may so say, a good Christian betwixt them; the latter whereof take the Soul and Spirit of Christianity, but cannot be acquitted of neglecting what is not less essential in the Doctrine of our Salvation; and that not only because what God has joyn'd Man cannot disjoyn; but also because it is an Eternal Verity, that such Creatures as we are, cannot consistently with the Attributes of God, any other way than that of Justification by Faith, be intitled to Eternal Life. For the Dispensation of the Gospel is not a meerly Arbitrary thing; but is the result of Infinite Wisdom, and Goodness, for the Salvation of Men. And if the Beauty and Harmony of its Divine Contrivance is not to all Men evident, it is because they search not for the Christian Religion purely, as it is deliver'd in the Scriptures, but take it up together with the mixtures of Humane inventions, and

40

conceits; wherein Additions and Substractions have been made to the Truth of God, at Mens Pleasure: Whose several Systems and Notions, whilst every one yet indeavours to support by Scripture Authority, many become thereby discourag'd from the study of those Holy Oracles, as being perswaded from hence that the Bible is (at best) a Book too difficult to be understood by them; if not truly, a Rhapsodie of contradictions, that may be brought alike to assert any thing that shall come into Men's Fancies to prove from thence.

What then should those who would cure, or prevent all Mistakes prejudicial to the right understanding the Christian Religion so carefully do, as to perswade and ingage People diligently and with unprejudic'd Minds to study the Scriptures; and not (as is usual) to embrace Opinions concerning Religion first, and then consult the Scriptures only to fortifie from thence their preconceiv'd Sentiments? for doing thus they do in effect, but rely blindly upon the Teachings of Men, and such Men too (as God knows have themselves for the most part) as blindly follow'd others; whilst here and there some few (as having more refin'd Wits, and disdaining such Shackles as the generality like to wear, yet not loving the Truth in the Simplicity thereof) have sought to improve and adorn it by their Philosophical Conceits, and Notions; a Thing no less dangerous than the Former. For to such as are better pleas'd with curious Speculations, than plain and obvious Verities, it is very apt to happen that a Favourite Hypothesis, or Opinion, shall run quite away with their Reason and Judgment: which when it does, the Scriptures are sure to be interpreted with conformity to that as if it were an Eternal, and Unquestionable Principle of Truth. And thus too often is it seen that the Sacred Doctrines of Divine Revelation are submitted to be try'd by Philosophical Fancies, as a Criterion of their Truth; which is truly a more direct disservice to Christianity than the above-mentioned implicite Faith, since this evidently exposes even the Divine Authority of the Christian Religion to be question'd. For when any, especially if such whose profession it is to be Teachers of this Religion, shall either argue against the plain Sense of what is deliver'd in the Scriptures, meerly because it is not reconcileable to their preconceiv'd Sentiments: or to those of their Admir'd Masters of Reason; or else shall insist upon some of their own or these Mens Theorems as necessary to be believ'd in confirmation of any thing taught by our Saviour, or his Apostles; what can the Natural effect of this be, but to make such as have not the leisure, or inclination to examine the Truth of this Revelation, Sceptical in regard thereof; by perswading them that those themselves who are rational Men amongst the very Teachers of the Christian Religion, are not very clearly and fully convinc'd of its Divine Authority; since if they were, they would certainly submit their Opinions to be try'd by the Scriptures, and not warp the Scriptures to a compliance with their Opinions; or think the Doctrines contain'd in them needed any other confirmation to support them. And wherefore must it be thought that such Men, as these, are not convinc'd of the divine Revelation of the Christian Religion, but from hence, that they (who will be presum'd to have examin'd this matter the best of any Men) do find indeed some flaw or just cause of doubt in the evidence thereof? From whence it is that they prefer their Natural Reason as a surer Teacher than that Revelation; however on some occasions they speak highly of it. And as Men of this Philosophical Genius have usually more Vertue than those who hoodwink'd follow their Leaders; or than such who look upon Vertue as no part of Religion; there will, on this account, as also for the Reputation of their uncommon Science, be probably a distinguishing esteem had of such: Whence the apparent want of deference in these Men to the Scriptures (liable to be look'd upon as some degree of Scepticism) is of dangerous Example; which is obviously manifest in that direct tendency this has to satisfie those in their infidelity, who cannot, or will not, find leisure to examine for themselves the Truths of Religion. But there is also a farther ill influence which apparent want of deference to Scripture Authority in those who pretend to believe (and, much more, to teach the Gospel) has: And that is to the countenanceing too much that Multitude who preferring the Christian Religion, do in their Practical that which these Men do in their Speculative Opinions, *viz.* make the dictates of the Gospel their Rule so far only, as they are vouch'd for and Authoriz'd by their Reason, infected, as it is, by Custom, Passion, or Worldly Interest; which is done by very many who would be offended to have their belief of the Scriptures Question'd. But however they profess to own them, none who act thus can be rationally thought to be sincerely perswaded of their divine Authority, altho' it is possible that many such Men may have no intire disbelief thereof neither; it being barely not assenting, which is the Natural Effect of Ignorance in those who have good Sense enough to see that it is irrational, to be confidently assur'd of what they have not sufficient Reason to be so assur'd of.

Now this want of a firm assent to the Divine Authority of the Scriptures in such as yet profess to own them for the word of God, is unquestionably evident when such Men acquiesce not in the Precepts of the Gospel, as the Rule of their Actions, any farther than they find those Precepts to be Authoriz'd by the Testimony of their Reason: Of which manner of acting many very common examples may be easily brought.

It is true that how much soever a Man is perswaded of the Authority of any Rule, a strong Passion, or Apparent Interest may yet seduce him from the Obedience due to its prescriptions; but such a Transgression being accompanied with Regret, or followed with Repentance, the Rule is still as much acknowledg'd as if it were obey'd; and none, on the score of a contrary practice, are chargeable with a disbelief thereof, but such who do, on a deliberate Choice and without Remorse, transgress against it; which many professing to be Christians not only themselves do, but even teach their Children the like: in which latter case it cannot be suppos'd that they are misled by the strength of any prevailing Passion.

That we should forgive our Enemies and be patient under injuries (for instance) are, as plainly as words can make them so, commanded in the Scriptures; yet how many are there professing to believe that the Scriptures are the Word of God, who, as if no such Commands as these were deliver'd by Christ, or his Disciples, do both Practice and Teach, the not putting up Affronts unreveng'd; and this only because the Fashion of the Country has establish'd it, that a Gentleman cannot do so with *Honour*? A Term which herein signifies nothing, but agreeably to certain measures of acting that Men have Arbitrarily made for themselves, and which are not founded upon any Principle of right Reason; however to be obey'd, it seems, by a Gentleman preferably to the Commands of Christ. If there are Cases wherein from want of a due provision in Governments against some sort of Injuries it may be thought that Men are excusable in asserting their own Cause, yet thus much is at the least certain, That this Precept of Forgiveness could not be transgress'd against, as it very frequently is, by Men professing to believe the Authority of the Scriptures, if such were indeed fully perswaded that it was a divine Command which prohibited the avenging of our selves.

But others there are (contrary to these Men) who would find it altogether condemnable for a Man to hazard his own, and anothers Life in a Duel, or Rencounter (tho' caus'd by the Transport of ever so just a provocation) who would see no Evil in his mispending of his Time, consuming Day after Day, and Year after Year, uselesly to himself, or others, in a course of continual Idleness and Sauntring; as if he was made only to Eat and to Drink, or to gratifie his Senses. And how few Parents are there of Quality, even among such as are esteem'd the most vertuous, who do not permit their Daughters to pass the best part of their Youth in that Ridiculous Circle of Diversions, which is pretty generally thought the proper business of Young Ladies; and which so ingrosses them that they can find no spare Hours, wherein to make any such improvements of their understanding, as the leisure which they have for it exacts from them as rational Creatures; or as is requisite or useful to the discharging well their present, or future Duties?

Some formal Devotions are (perhaps) necessary to some of These, to preserve them even in their own good esteem; and they that can regularly find half an Hour, or an Hour in a Day to employ in private upon this, and in reading some pious Book, together with, it may be, a certain Number of Chapters in the Bible, need nothing more to make them be cry'd up for great examples to the Age they live in; as if all this while there were no Precepts for these People in the Gospel, concerning the improvement of their Time, and Talents, as things whereof they must one Day be accountable. For others it may be they cannot but see that there are such Commands; but the Sacred Law of Fashion has made endless Idle Visits, and less Innocent Entertainments, the indispensibly constant Employment of those of their Condition: and when they are grown Old in the perpetually repeated round of such Impertinence and Folly, they have but labour'd much in their Calling.

Another Instance how little many, who profess to believe the Scriptures, do apparently look upon them as the Rule of their Actions, we have in regard of the Precept *not to Covet*; which is as much forbidden by the Law of God as *not to Steal*, or Cozen a Man of what is his property: And yet the same Parents who have bred their Children in such a Sense of the Enormity of these last Vices, as that they oftentimes seem to them like things that they are Naturally uncapable of, are so far from teaching them to restrain their Exorbitant Desires, that very oft they themselves with care inspire these into them: Whence it is sufficiently clear that the difference made between Stealing and Cheating, or Coveting (alike forbidden by the Law of God) is from hence, That Ambition is thought a Passion becoming some Ranks of Men, but Cheating or Stealing not Vices proper for a Gentleman. A distinction that must needs refer to some other Rule than that of the Gospel; which therefore is not

That which, as a Divine Law, does prescribe to such Men the Measures of their Actions.

To bring but one instance more of the Commands of Christ being comply'd with but so far only, as they do comply with some other Rule prefer'd thereto by such as yet pretend to be Christians; *Chastity* (for example) is, according to the Gospel, a Duty to both Sexes, yet a Transgression herein, even with the aggravation of wronging another Man, and possibly a whole Family thereby, is ordinarily talk'd as lightly of, as if it was but a Peccadillo in a Young Man, altho' a far less Criminal Offence against this Duty in a Maid shall in the Opinion of the same Persons brand her with perpetual Infamy: The nearest Relations oftentimes are hardly brought to look upon her after such a dishonour done by her to their Family; whilst the Fault of her more guilty Brother finds but a very moderate reproof from them; and in a little while, it may be, becomes the Subject of their Mirth and Raillery. And why still is this wrong plac'd distinction made, but because there are measures of living establish'd by Men themselves according to a conformity, or disconformity with which, and not with the Precepts of Jesus Christ, their Actions are measur'd, & judg'd of? A thing which would be unaccountable if Men were indeed heartily perswaded of the Divine Revelation of our Saviours Doctrine; and did not profess to believe this but because it is the Fashion of their Country so to do; and that their Parents have done so before them; or, at most, that possibly they may have receiv'd from their Education some impressions which will not permit them to reject the Christian Religion, any more than firmly induce their Assent to the Truth of it.

That Men who have any Vertue, or Sobriety, and who are not intirely destitute of good Sense, can suffer in themselves such an uncertainty about what is of so great moment to them as the Truths of the Christian Religion, is indeed strange; but as the slightest Arguments against any Truth have some weight to those who know not the Evidence of that Truth, so also such as have never been accustom'd, whilst Young, to exercise themselves in any Rational Inquiry, do usually in a more advanc'd Age look upon the easiest Labour of this kind as painful: And thence (for the most part) do either lazily think it best to acquiesce, as well as they can, in such Mens Sentiments as they have imagin'd the best to understand this matter; or else are readily inclin'd from the disagreement, and contrariety of Peoples thoughts about it, to take a Resolution of not troubling themselves at all concerning it; as being a thing wherein there is no certainty to be found, and probably therefore but little Truth: An Opinion which the too commonly avow'd Scepticism of the Age helps much to confirm unthinking People in; and that the more, because to doubt of what the most believe (tho' few have any other Reason for so doubting but that others do not doubt) has very much prevail'd in our Days to intitle Men to the Reputation of more than ordinary Wit and Sagacity. But the Scepticism among us has truly been so far from being the effect of uncommon Light, and Knowledge; as that it has been, and is much owing to the preceding fashionableness of a very general Ignorance, both in regard of Religion, and also of other useful Sciences; for Men's not knowing how profitably, and with pleasure to employ their Time, is apparently one great cause of their Debauchery; and so long as the Consciousness and Shame of not acting like rational Creatures is not extinguished in them, the uneasiness of that remorse puts them Naturally upon seeking out Principles to justifie their Conduct upon; few Men being able to indure the constant Reproaches of their own Reason: Whence if they do not conform their Actions to the dictates of that, they will Naturally indeavour to warp their Reason to a compliance with their practices: A reconcilement one way, or other, between these, being necessary to the making Men, that are not very profligate indeed, in good conceit, or even at Peace with themselves.

By that want of Knowledge which I have ventur'd to say is fashionable, I understand not only ignorance among Men, who have leisure for it, of Arts and Sciences in general; but also, and especially the want of such particular Knowledge as is requisite to every one for the well discharging either their Common or peculiar Business and Duty; wherein Religion is necessarily included, as being the Duty of all Persons to understand, of whatever Sex, Condition, or Calling they are of. Now to affirm that the greater part of People are ignorant concerning that which is not only their Duty to know, but which also many are so sensible they ought to know, as that they pretend to understand it enough to be either zealous about, or else to contemn it; and to assert likewise that they want the knowledge of what is peculiarly belonging to them, in their particular Station, to understand; are such Charges as ought not to be alledg'd, if they are not so evidently true, as that we cannot open our Eyes without seeing them to be so.

In respect of Religion, it is, I think, universally allow'd to be true of the common People of all sorts (tho' surely not without Matter of Reproach to some, or other, whose Care their better Instruction ought to be) that they are very ignorant. But we will consider here only such superior Ranks of Persons, in reference to whom what has already been said, has been spoken: And to begin with the Female Sex, who certainly ought to be Christians; how many of these, comparatively, may it be presum'd that there are, from the meanest Gentlewoman to the greatest Ladies, that can give any such account of the Christian Religion, as would inform an inquisitive Stranger what it consisted in; and what are the grounds of believing it? Such Women as understand something of the distinguishing Opinions of that Denomination they have been bred up in, are commonly thought highly intelligent in Religion; but I think there are but very few, even of this little number, who could well inform a rational Heathen concerning Christianity itself: Which is an Ignorance inexcusable in them, tho', perhaps, it is very often the effect only of the want of other useful Knowledge, for the not having whereof, Women are much more to be pitty'd than blam'd.

The improvements of Reason, however requisite to Ladies for their Accomplishment, as rational Creatures; and however needful to them for the well Educating of their Children, and to their being useful in their Families, yet are rarely any recommendation of them to Men; who foolishly thinking, that Money will answer to all things, do, for the most part, regard nothing else in the Woman they would Marry: And not often finding what they do not look for, it would be no wonder if their Off-spring should inherit no more Sense than themselves. But be Nature ever so kind to them in this respect, yet through want of cultivating the Tallents she bestows upon those of the Female Sex, her Bounty is usually lost upon them; and Girls, betwixt silly Fathers and ignorant Mothers, are generally so brought up, that traditionary Opinions are to them, all their lives long, instead of Reason. They are, perhaps, sometimes told in regard of what Religion exacts, That they must *Believe* and *Do* such and such things, because the Word of God requires it; but they are not put upon searching the Scriptures for themselves, to see whether, or no, these things are so; and they so little know why they should look upon the Scriptures to be the Word of God, that but too often they are easily perswaded out of the Reverence due to them as being so: And (if they happen to meet with such bad examples) are not seldom brought from thence, even to scoff at the Documents of their Education; and, in consequence thereof, to have no Religion at all. Whilst others (naturally more dispos'd to be Religious) are either (as divers in the Apostles Days were) *carry'd away with every wind of Doctrine, ever learning and never coming to the knowledge of the Truth*; Weak, Superstitious, Useless Creatures; or else, if more tenacious in their Natures, blindly and conceitedly wedded to the Principles and Opinions of their Spiritual Guides; who having the direction of their Consciences, rarely fail to have that also of their Affairs and Fortunes. A Wife of which sort proves, very often, no small unhappiness to the Family where she comes; for this kind of ignorant Persons are, of all others, the most Arrogant; and when they are once intitl'd to Saintship for their blind Zeal, as nothing is more troublesome than they in finding fault with, and censuring every one that differs from them, so to their Admirers (who lead them as they please) they think they can never pay enough for that Incence which is offer'd them: The dearest Interests of Humane Life being, oftentimes, thus sacrific'd to a vain Image of Piety; *whilst makers of long Prayers* have *devour'd Widows Houses.*

But what is here said implying that Ladies should so well understand their Religion, as to be able to answer both to such who oppose, and to such who misrepresent it; this may seem, perhaps, to require that they should have the Science of Doctors, and be well skill'd in Theological Disputes and Controversies; than the Study of which I suppose there could scarce be found for them a more useless Employment. But whether such Patrons of Ignorance as know nothing themselves which they ought to know, will call it Learning, or not, to understand the Christian Religion, and the grounds of receiving it; it is evident that they who think so much knowledge, as that, to be needless for a Woman, must either not be perswaded of the Truth of Christianity; or else must believe that Women are not concern'd to be Christians. For if Christianity be a Religion from God, and Women have Souls to be sav'd as well as Men; to know what this Religion consists in, and to understand the grounds on which it is to be receiv'd, can be no more than necessary Knowledge to a Woman, as well as to a Man: Which necessary Knowledge is sufficient to inable any one so far to answer to the Opposers or Corrupters of Christianity, as to secure them from the danger of being impos'd upon by such Mens Argumentations; which is all that I have thought requisite for a Lady; and not that she should be prepar'd to challenge every Adversary to Truth.

Now that thus much knowledge requires neither Learned Education, or great Study, to the attaining of it, appears in that the first Christians were mean and illiterate People; to which part of Mankind the Gospel may rather be thought to have had a more especial regard than that they are any way excluded from the Benefits thereof by incapacity in them to receive it. In the Apostles Days *there were not many Wise who were call'd*, and he tells us that *after that the World by Wisdom knew not God: it pleased God by the foolishness of Preaching to save them that believe*, and tho' *to the perfect* the same Apostle says, he did *Preach Wisdom*, yet it was the simplicity and plainness of the Christian Religion that made it *to the Jews a stumbling block, and to the Greeks foolishness.* From whence, we see that all Theorems too abstruse for Vulgar Apprehensions, which Christianity is believ'd to Teach, however Divine Truths, are yet no part of the Doctrine of Salvation. There is not therefore this pretence to impose upon any one the belief of any thing which they do not find to be reveal'd in Scripture; the doing of which, has not only caus'd deplorable dissentions among Christians, but also been an occasion to multitudes of well meaning People of having so confus'd and unsatisfactory conceptions and apprehensions concerning the Christian Religion as tho' perhaps not absolutely, or immediately prejudicial to their Salvation, yet are so to their seeing clearly that Christianity is a rational Religion; without which few will be very secure from the infection of Scepticism, or Infidelity, where those are become fashionable, and prevailing. A danger to which many Women are no less expos'd than Men, and oftentimes, more so. Whence it is but needful that they should so well understand their Religion as to be Christians upon the Convictions of their Reason; which is indeed no more than one would think it became every Christian, as a rational Creature, to be; were this not requisite in regard of Scepticism, and Infidelity, as to some it is not; there being, no doubt, many a Country Gentlewoman who has never in her Life heard Question'd, or once imagined that any one in their Wits could Question the Articles of her Faith; which yet she her self knows not why she believes.

From the too Notorious Truth of what has been said in reference to the little that Women know concerning Religion, it must be granted that the generality of them are shamefully Ignorant herein. As for other Science, it is believ'd so improper for, and is indeed so little allow'd them, that it is not to be expected from them: but the cause of this is only the Ignorance of Men.

The Age, we live in, has been, not undeservedly, esteem'd a knowing one: But to the Learned Clergy much has been owing for its having obtain'd that Character; and tho' some few Gentlemen have been the greatest advancers of Learning amongst us; yet they are very rare who apply themselves to any Science that is curious: And as for such knowledge as is no less than requisite for Men of Families, and Estates to have in regard of the proper business of their Station; it may, I think, be said that never was this more neglected than at present; since there is not a commoner complaint in every County than of the want of Gentlemen Qualified for the Service of their Country, *viz.* to be Executors of the Law, and Law Makers; both of which it belonging to this Rank of English Men to be, some insight into the Law which they are to see Executed, and into that Constitution which they are to support, cannot but be necessary to their well dischargeing these Trusts: Nor will this Knowledge be sufficiently Servicable to the Ends herein propos'd, without some Acquaintance likewise with History, Politicks, and Morals. Every one of these then are parts of Knowledge which an English Gentleman cannot, without blame, be Ignorant of, as being essential to the duly Qualifying him for what is his proper business.

But whether we farther look upon such Men as having Immortal Souls that shall be for ever Happy or Miserable, as they comply with the Terms which their Maker has propos'd to them; or whether we regard them as Protestants, whose Birthright it is not blindly to *Believe*, but to Examine their Religion; Or consider them only as Men whose ample Fortunes allow them leisure for so important a Study, they are without doubt oblig'd to understand the Religion they profess. Adding this then to what it is above concluded a Gentleman ought to know, let us examine how common such Knowledge only is amongst our Gentlemen, as we see, without just matter of Reproach to them, they cannot want: No one, I think, will deny that so much knowledge as this is so little ordinary, as that those are apparently the far greater number who have never consider'd any part hereof as an Acquisition, which they ought to make; and that they are but a few comparatively, and pass among us for Men extraordinary, who have but a competent knowledge in any one of the above-mention'd things.

What is by the Obligations of their Duty exacted from them in this regard, seems to be very little reflected on by them; and as for other Considerations, which, as Gentlemen, might be thought to induce them, their Ancestors care has distinguish'd them from their Tenants, and other inferior Neighbours, by Titles and Riches; and that is all the distinction which they desire to have; believing it, in respect of Knowledge, sufficient, if they did once understand a little Latin or Logick in the University; which whoso still retains, altho' he has made no use thereof to the real improvement of his understanding, is yet thought very highly accomplish'd, and passes (in the Country) for Learned.

As to Religion, by the little which most Gentlemen understand of that, and by the no shame which they ordinarily enough have in avowing this their ignorance, one cannot but suppose that it is pretty commonly thought by them a matter, the understanding whereof does not concern them: That the Publick has provided others to do this for them: And that their part herein is but to maintain (so far as by their Authority they can) what those Men assert.

Thus wretchedly destitute of all that Knowledge which they ought to have, are (generally speaking) our English Gentlemen: And being so, what wonder can it be, if they like not that Women should have Knowledge; for this is a quality that will give some sort of superiority even to those who care not to have it? But such Men as these would assuredly find their account much better therein, if tenderness of that Prerogative would teach them a more legitimate way of maintaining it, than such a one as is a very great impediment or discouragement, at the least, to others in the doing what God requires of them. For it is an undeniable Truth that a Lady who is able but to give an account of her Faith, and to defend her Religion against the attaques of the Cavilling Wits of the Age; or the Abuses of the Obtruders of vain Opinions: That is capable of instructing her Children in the reasonableness of the Christian Religion; and of laying in them the Foundations of a solid Vertue; that a Lady (I say) no more knowing than this does demand, can hardly escape being call'd Learned by the Men of our days; and in consequence thereof, becoming a Subject of Ridicule to one part of them, and of Aversion to the other; with but a few exceptions of some vertuous and rational Persons. And is not the incuring of general dislike, one of the strongest discouragements that we can have to any thing?

If the assistance of Mothers be, as I have already affirm'd it is, necessary to the right forming of the Minds, and regulating of the Manners of their Children; I am not in the wrong in reckoning (as I do) that this care is indispensibly a Mothers Duty. Now it cannot, I think, be doubted, but that a Mothers Concurrence and Care is thus necessary, if we consider that this is a work which can never be too soon begun, it being rarely at all well performed, if not betimes undertaken; nothing being so effectual to the making Men vertuous, as to have good Habits and Principles of Vertue establish'd in them before the Mind is tainted with any thing opposite or prejudicial hereunto. Those therefore must needs much over-look the chief Business of Education, or have little consider'd the Constitution of Humane Nature, that reckon for nothing the first eight or ten Years of a Boys Life; an Age wherein Fathers, who seldom are able to do it at any time, can neither charge themselves with the care of their Children, nor be the watchful inspectors of those that they must be trusted to; who usually and unavoidably by most Parents, are a sort of People far fitter to be Learners than Teachers of the Principles of Vertue and Wisdom; the great Foundation of both which consists in being able to govern our Passions, and subject our Appetites to the direction of our Reason: A Lesson hardly ever well learnt, if it be not taught us from our very Cradles. To do which requires no less than a Parents Care and Watchfulness; and therefore ought undoubtedly to be the Mothers business to look after, under whose Eye they are. An exemption from which, Quality (even of the highest degree) cannot give; since the Relation between the Mother and Child is equal amongst all Ranks of People. And it is a very preposterous Abuse of Quality to make it a pretence for being unnatural. This is a Truth which perhaps would displease many Ladies were it told them, and therefore, probably, it is that they so seldom hear it: But none of them could be so much offended with any one for desiring hereby to restrain them from some of their expensive and ridiculous Diversions, by an employment so worthy of Rational Creatures, and so becoming of maternal tenderness, as it is just to be with them for neglecting their Children: A Fault that women of Quality are every way too often guilty of, and are perhaps more without excuse for, than for any other that they are ordinarily taxable with. For tho' it is to be fear'd that few Ladies (from the disadvantage of their own Education) are so well fitted as they ought to be, to take the care of their Children, yet not to be willing to do what they can herein, either as thinking this a matter of too much pains for them, or below their Condition, expresses so senseless a Pride, and so much want of the affectionate and compassionate Tenderness natural to that Sex and Relation, that one would almost be tempted to question whether such Women were any more capable of, than worthy to be the Mothers of Rational Creatures.

But natural Affection apart, it should be consider'd by these, that no one is Born into the World to live idly; enjoying the Fruit and Benefit of other Peoples Labours, without contributing reciprocally some way or other, to the good of the Community answerably to that Station wherein God (the common Father of all) has plac'd them; who has evidently intended Humane kind for Society and mutual Communion, as Members of the same Body, useful every one each to other in their respective places. Now in what can Women whose Condition puts them above all the

Necessities or Cares of a mean or scanty Fortune, at once so honourably and so usefully, both to themselves and others, be employ'd in as in looking after the Education and Instruction of their own Children? This seems indeed to be more particularly the Business and Duty of such than of any others: And if example be necessary to perswade them that they will not herein do any thing mis-becoming their Rank, the greatest Ladies amongst us may be assur'd that those of a Condition superior to theirs, have heretofore been so far from thinking it any abasement to them to charge themselves with the instruction of their own Children, that (to their Immortal Honour) they have made it part of their Business to assist to that of other Peoples also, who were likely one day to be of consequence to the Common-wealth.

And could the bare Love of their Country induce, among many more, the great *Cornelia*, Mother of the *Gracchi*, and *Aurelia* the Mother of *Julius Cæsar*, to do this for the Sons of Noble-men of *Rome* to whom they had no Relation but that of their common Country, and shall not the like consideration, or what is infinitely beyond this, that of their Children being hereafter for ever happy or miserable, accordingly as they live in this World, prevail with the Ladies of our Days, who call themselves Christians, to employ some of their Time and Pains upon their own Off-spring? The care of which (as has been said) should begin with the first Years of Childrens Lives, in curbing at the earliest appearance thereof, every their least evil inclination; and accustoming them to an absolute, constant, and universal Submission and Obedience to the Will of those who have the disposal of them: Since they will hardly ever after (especially in a great Fortune) be govern'd by their own Reason, who are not made supple to that of others, before they are able to judge of fit and unfit, by any other measure than as it is the Will, or not, of such whom they believe to have a just Power over them. As they do become capable of examining and determining their Actions by Reason, they should be taught never to do any thing of consequence heedlesly; and to look upon the Dictates of their Reason as so inviolable a Rule of their Determinations, that no Passion or Appetite must ever make them swerve therefrom.

But instead of following this Method, it is commonly thought too soon to correct Children for any thing, 'till the Season is past for this sort of Discipline; which, if it come too late, is commonly so far from producing the good it was design'd for, that losing the benefit of Correction (which, if duly apply'd, is of infinite use) it turns to a Provocation; and renders stiff and incorrigible a Temper it was meant to supple. Nor is it seldom that through this wrong tim'd Discipline, together with that remisness and inequality wherewith Childrens Inclinations are over-rul'd, their Parents Government over them seems to them not a Natural, and just right establish'd for their benefit, but a Tyrannick and Arbritary Power, which accordingly they without Remorse disobey, whenever they believe that they can do so with Impunity: And what is still worse, their evil Dispositions, for the most part, are not only not timely enough restrain'd, but Children are actually taught to indulge to their naturally irregular Inclinations, by those Vicious or wretchedly ignorant People, who are plac'd about them; and who almost universally instil down-right Vice into them, even before they can well speak; as Revenge, Covetousness, Pride and Envy: Whilst the silly Creatures who do them so unspeakable Mischiefs are scarce capable of being made to understand the harm that they do; but think Parents ill-natur'd, or that they have fancies fit only to be smil'd at, who will deny their Child a thing for no other reason, it may be, but because he has desir'd it: And who before he is trusted to go alone will check his Resentment, Impatience, Avarice, or Vanity, which they think becomes him so prettily; neither will suffer him to be rewarded for doing what they bid him to do.

This I am sure, that who so has try'd how very little Sense is to be met with, or can be infus'd into Nurses, and Nurse-Maids; and with what difficulty even the best of them by those who make it their business to watch over them, are restrain'd from what they are perswaded has no hurt in it, will soon be satisfy'd how little fit it is to trust Children any more than is necessary, in such Hands. And no wiser than such, if not much worse, are the greatest part of those who are usually their immediate Successors, *viz.* young Scholars and French Maids, erected into Tutors and Governesses, only for the sake of a little Latin and French.

In Mr. L—— s excellent *Treatise of Education*, he shews how early and how great a Watchfulness and Prudence are requisite to the forming the Mind of a Child to Vertue; and whoso shall read what he has writ on that Subject, will, it is very likely, think that few Mothers are qualify'd for such an undertaking as this: But that they are not so is the Fault which should be amended: In the mean time nevertheless, their presum'd willingness to be in the right, where the Happiness of their Children is concerned in it, must certainly inable them, if they were but once convinc'd that this was their Duty, to perform it much better than such People will do, who have as little Skill and Ability for it as themselves; and who besides, that they rarely desire to learn any more than they have, are not induc'd by Affection to do for those under their care all the Good that they can. Since then the Affairs either of Men's Callings, or of their private Estates, or the Service of their Country (all which are indispensibly their Business) allows them not the leisure to look daily after the Education of their Children; and that, otherwise, also they are naturally less capable than Women of that Complaisance and Tenderness, which the right Instruction and Direction of that Age requires; and since Servants are so far from being fit to be rely'd upon in that great concern, that to watch against the Impediments they actually bring thereto, is no small part of the care that a wise Parent has to take; I do presume that (ordinarily speaking) this so necessary a Work of forming betimes the Minds of Children so as to dispose them to be hereafter Wise and Vertuous Men and Women, cannot be perform'd but by Mothers only. It being a thing practicable but by a very few to purchase the having always Wise, Vertuous and well Bred People, to take the place of a Parent in governing their Children; and together with them such Servants and Teachers, as must peculiarly be employ'd about them; For the World does not necessarily abound with such Persons as these, and in such circumstances as not to pretend to more profitable employments than Men of one or two thousand Pounds a Year (and much less those great numbers who have smaller Estates) can often afford to make the care of governing their Children from their Infancy to be. The procuring of such a Person as this may (by accident) sometimes be in such a ones Power; but to propose the ingaging for reward whenever there shall be need for them, vertuous, wife, and well-bred Men and Women, to spend their time in taking care of the Education of young Children, is what can be done but by a very few; since the doing this would not be found an easy charge to the greater part of almost any rank amongst us; unless they would be content for the sake hereof to abridge themselves of some of their extravagant Expences; which are usually the last that Men will deny themselves.

It is indeed wonderful (if we consider Men as rational Creatures) to see how much Mony they will often bestow, not upon their Vices only, (for this is not so unaccountable) but upon meerly fashionable Vanities, which give them more Trouble than Pleasure in the enjoyment: Yet at the same time be as sparing, as is possible, of cost upon a Child's Education; and it is certain, that for Rewards considerable enough to make it worth their while, those of a far different Character from such as for the most part undertake it, would be induc'd to accept even the early charge of Childrens Instruction. But every Gentleman of a good Family, or good Estate also, is not in Circumstances to propound such sufficient Rewards; and for what the most can afford to give, very few capable of performing this matter well, will trouble themselves about it; at least with such Pupils as must be attended with Nurses or Maids. Wherefore no other remedy, I believe, can be found but in returning still to our Conclusion, That this great concernment, on which no less than Peoples Temporal and Eternal Happiness does mightily depend, ought to be the Care and Business of Mothers. Nor do Women seem less peculiarly adapted by Nature hereunto, than it can be imagin'd they should be, if the Author of Nature (as no doubt he did) design'd this to be their Province in that division of Cares of Humane Life, which ought to be made between a Man and his Wife. For that softness, gentleness and tenderness, natural to the Female Sex, renders them much more capable than Men are of such an insinuating Condescention to the Capacities of young Children, as is necessary in the Instruction and Government of them, insensibly to form their early Inclinations. And surely these distinguishing Qualities of the Sex were not given barely to delight, when they may, so manifestly, be profitable also, if joyn'd with a well informed Understanding: From whence, *viz.* from Womans being naturally thus fitted to take this care of their little Ones, it follows, that besides the injustice done to themselves thereby, it is neglecting the Direction of Nature for the well breeding up of Children, when Ladies are render'd uncapable hereof, through the want of such due improvements of their Reason as are requisite hereunto.

That this has been no more reflected upon from a Principle of Pitty to that tender Age of Children which so much requires help, seems very strange: For what can move a juster Commiseration than to see such poor innocents, so far from having the Aid they stand in need of, that even those who the most wish to do them good, and who resent, with the deepest Compassion, every little Malady which afflicts their Bodies, do never attempt to rescue them from the greatest evils which attend them in this Life, but even themselves assist to plunge them therein, by cherishing in them those Passions which will inevitably render them miserable? A thing which can never be otherwise whilst Women are bred up in no right Notions of Religion and Vertue; or to know any use of Reason but in the service of their Passions and Inclinations; or at best of their (comparatively trivial) Interests.

To assert upon this occasion, that Ladies would do well, if, before they came to the care of Families, they did imploy some of their many idle Hours in gaming a little Knowledge in Languages, and the useful Sciences, would be, I know, to contradict the Sense of most Men; but yet, I think, that such an Assertion admits of no other Confutation than the usual one which opposite Opinions to theirs are wont to receive from People who Reason not, but live by Fancy, and Custom; *viz.* being laugh'd at:

For it cannot be deny'd that this Knowledge would hereafter be more, or less, useful to Ladies, in inabling them either themselves to teach their Children, or better to over-see and direct, those who do so: And tho' Learning is perhaps the least part in Education, it is not to be neglected; but even betimes taken some care of, least a Habit of Idleness, or Inapplication of the Mind be got, which once contracted, is very hardly cur'd.

This being so, and that the beginnings of all Science are difficult to Children (who cannot like grown People fix their Attention) it is justly to befear'd that they should by the ill usage they receive from the impatience and peevishness of such Teachers, as Servants, or Young Tutors, take an Aversion to Learning (and we see in effect, that this very frequently happens). For the Teaching of little Children so as not to disgust them, does require much greater Patience and Address, than common People are often capable of; or than most can imagine, who have not had experience hereof. But should such Teachers as we have spoke of, have the necessary complaisance for those they Teach, there is then, on the other side, a yet greater danger to be apprehended from them, which is that their Pupils will become fond of them; the bad effect of which will be, That by an Affectation Natural in Children of imitating those they Love, they will have their Manners and Dispositions Tinctur'd and Tainted by those of Persons so dear to them.

Now both the inconveniences here mention'd, might, at least in great measure, if not wholly, be Remedy'd, would Mothers but be at so much Pains as to Teach their Children either altogether, or in good part themselves, what it is fit for them to learn in the first Eight or Ten Years of their Lives. As to Read English perfectly; To understand ordinary Latin; and Arithmetick; with some general knowledge of Geography, Chronology, and History. Most, or all of which things may at the above-said Age be understood by a Child of a very ordinary capacity; and may be so taught Children as that they may learn them almost insensibly in Play, if they have skilful Teachers: It seems to me therefore that Young Ladies cannot better employ so much of their Time as is requisite hereto, than in acquiring such Qualifications as these, which may be of so great use to them hereafter; however, if any who have not made this early Provision of such Science, are yet truly desirous to do their Children all the good that is in their Power to do them, they may, tho' not with the same Facility, yet be able to instruct them alike, notwithstanding that disadvantage; and Mr. L—— on the Experience thereof, has asserted, That a Mother who understands not Latin before hand, may yet teach it to her Child; which, if she can, it is not to be doubted but that she may do the same of all the rest; for such a Superficial Knowledge as will serve to enter any one in every of the above-named Sciences, is much easier attain'd than the Latin Tongue; and if a Mother have ever so little more Capacity than her Child, she may easily keep before him, in teaching both him and her self together; whereby she will make herself the best Reparation that she can for her past neglect, or that of her Parents herein: Who yet, perhaps, not from negligence may have declin'd giving her this advantage. For Parents sometimes do purposely omit it from an apprehension that should their Daughters be perceiv'd to understand any learned Language, or be conversant in Books, they might be in danger of not finding Husbands; so few Men, as do, relishing these accomplishments in a Lady. Nor, probably, would even the example of a Mother herself who was thus qualify'd, and likewise understood, as is afore-said, her Religion, be any great incouragement to her Daughters to imitate her example, but the contrary. For this Knowledge, one part whereof is so strictly the Duty of a Christian, and the other so inconsiderable to those whose Time commonly lies upon their Hands, would in itself, or in the consequences of it, expose a young Woman of Quality (especially if not thought unfit for the fashionable Commerce of the World) to be characteriz'd or censur'd, as would not be very pleasing to her. For if it be consider'd, that she who did seriously desire to make the best use of what she knew, would necessarily be oblig'd (for the gaining of Time wherein she might do so) to order the Course, and manner of her Life something differently from others of her Sex and Condition, it cannot be doubted but that a Conduct, which carry'd with it so much Reproach to Woman's Idleness, and disappointment to Men's Vanity, would quickly be judg'd fit to be ridicul'd out of the World before others were infected by the example. So that the best Fate which a Lady thus knowing, and singular, could expect, would be that hardly escaping Calumny, she should be in Town the Jest of the *Would-be-Witts*; tho wonder of Fools, and a Scarecrow to keep from her House many honest People who are to be pitty'd for having no more Wit than they have, because it is not their own Fault that they have no more. But in the Country she would, probably, fare still worse; for there her understanding of the Christian Religion would go near to render her suspected of Heresy even by those who thought the best of her: Whilst her little Zeal for any Sect or Party would make the Clergy of all sorts give her out for a *Socinian* or a *Deist*: And should but a very little Philosophy be added to her other Knowledge, even for an Atheist. The Parson of the Parish, for fear of being ask'd hard Questions, would be shy of coming near her, were his Reception ever so inviting; and this could not but carry some ill intimation with it to such as Reverenc'd the Doctor, and who, it is likely, might be already satisfy'd from the Reports of Nurses, and Maids, that their Lady was indeed a Woman of very odd Whimsies. Her prudent Conduct and Management of her affairs would probably secure her from being thought out of her Wits by her near Neighbours; but the Country Gentlemen that wish'd her well, could not yet chuse but be afraid for her, lest too much Learning might in Time make her Mad.

The saving of but one Soul from Destruction, is, it is true, a noble recompense for ten Thousand such Censurers as these; but it is wondrous strange that only to be a Christian, with so much other Knowledge as a Child of Nine or Ten Years Old may, and ought to have, should expose a Lady to so great Reproaches; And what a shame is this for Men whose woful Ignorance is the alone Cause thereof? For it is manifestly true that if the inimitable Author of *Les Caracteres, ou les Moeurs de ce Siecle*, had demanded in *England, who forbids Knowledge to Women*? It must have been answer'd him, the Ignorance of the Men does so; and the same Answer I think he might have receiv'd in his own Country.

Monsieur Bruyere says indeed, and likely it is, *That Men have made no Laws, or put out any Edicts whereby Women are prohibited to open their Eyes; to Read; to Remember what they Read, and to make use thereof in their Conversation, or in composing of Works.* But surely he had little Reason to suppose, as he herein does, that Women could not otherwise than *by Laws and Edicts* be restrain'd from Learning. It is sufficient for this that no body assists them in it; and that they are made to see betimes that it would be disadvantageous to them to have it. For how few Men are there, that arrive to any Eminence therein? tho' Learning is not only not prohibited to them *by Laws and Edicts;* but that ordinarily much Care, and Pains, is taken to give it them; and that great Profits, oftentimes, and, always, Honour attends their having it.

The Law of Fashion, establish'd by Repute and Disrepute, is to most People the powerfullest of all Laws, as Monsieur *Bruyere* very well knew; whose too Satyrical Genius makes him assign as Causes of Womens not having Knowledge, the universally necessary consequences of being bred in the want thereof. But what on different occasions he says of the Sex, will either on the one part vindicate them, or else serve for an Instance that this Ingenious Writers Reflections, however witty, are not always instructive, or just Corrections. For either Women have generally some other more powerful Principle of their Actions than what terminates in rendering themselves pleasing to Men (as he insinuates they have not) or else they neglect the improvement of their Minds and Understandings, as not finding them of any use to that purpose; whence it is not equal in him to charge it peculiarly (as he does) upon that Sex (if it be indeed so much chargeable on them as on Men) that they are diverted from Science by *une curiosit toute differente de celle qui contente l'Espirt: ou un tout autre gout que celuy d'exercer leur Memoire.*

Yet since I think it is but Natural, and alike so in both Sexes, to desire to please the other, I may, I suppose, without any Injurious Reflexion upon Ladies, presume, that if Men did usually find Women the more amiable for being knowing, they would much more commonly, than now they are, be so.

But the Knowledge hitherto spoken of has a nobler Aim than the pleasing of Men, and begs only Toleration from them; in granting whereof they would at least equally consult their own advantage: as they could not but find, did They not by a common Folly, incident to Humane Nature, hope that contradictions should subsist together in their Favour; from whence only it is that very many who would not that Women should have Knowledge, do yet complain of, and very impatiently bear the Natural, and unavoidable consequences of their Ignorance.

But what sure Remedy can be found for Effects whose Cause remains? and on what ground can it be expected that Ignorance and uninstructed Persons should have the Venues which proceed from a rightly inform'd Understanding, and well cultivated Mind? or not be liable to those Vices which their Natures incline them to? And how should it otherwise be than that they, who have never consider'd the Nature and Constitution of Things, or weigh'd the Authority of the Divine Law, and what it exacts of them, should be perswaded that nothing can be so truly profitable to them as the Indulgence of their present Passions, and Appetites? Which whoso places their Happiness in the satisfaction of, cannot fail of being themselves miserable, or of making those so who are concern'd in them.

Humane Nature is not capable of durable satisfaction when the Passions and Appetites are not under the direction of right Reason: And whilst we eagerly pursue what disappoints our expectation, or cloys with the Enjoyment, as all irregular pleasures, however Natural, do; and whilst we daily create to our selves desires still more vain, as thinking thereby to be supply'd with new Delights, we shall ever (instead of finding true Contentment) be subjected to uneasiness, disgust and vexation: The unhappy state more, or less, of all who want that Knowledge which is requisite to direct their Actions suitably to the Ends which as rational Creatures they ought to propose: and as can inable them profitably to employ their Time.

But since Examples do the best perswade, let us see, with respect to Women, in the most considerable Instances, what plainly are the Natural consequences of that Ignorance which they usually are bred in; and which Men think so advantageous to themselves. We will suppose then a Lady bred, as the generality of Men think she should be, in a blind belief concerning Religion; and taught that it is even ridiculous for a Lady to trouble her Head about this matter; since it is so far from being a Science fit for her, that it indeed properly belongs only to Gown-Men: and that a Woman very well Merits to be laugh'd at who will act the Doctor: Her Duty in the case being plain and easie; as requiring only of her to believe and practice what she is taught at Church, or in such Books of Piety as shall be recommended to her by her Parents, or some Spiritual Director.

This is generally, I think, the Sense of Men concerning the Knowledge which Ladies ought to have of Religion: And thus much, I doubt not may suffice for their Salvation. But the saving of their Souls (tho' it were herein as sure as it is possible) is not, I suppose, all that Men are Solicitous for in regard of their Wives; their own Honour in that of those so near to them, does I think, much more frequently and sensibly employ their Care: And that, too often, appears to be but very weakly secur'd by such an implicit Faith as this. For these Believers (especially if they are thought to have any Wit, as well as Beauty) will hardly escape meeting some time or other, with those who will ask them *why they Believe*; and if they find then that they have no more Reason for going to Church than they should have had to go to Mass, or even to the Synagogue, had they been bred amongst Papists or Jews, they must needs, at the same time, doubt whether, or no, the Faith they have been brought up in, is any righter than either of these; from whence they will, (by easy steps) be induc'd to question the Truth of all Religion, when they shall be told by those who have insinuated themselves into their Esteem and good Graces, that indeed All Religions are, alike, the Inventions and Artifices of cunning Men to govern the World by; unworthy of imposing upon such as have their good Sense: That Fools only, and Ignorants are kept in Awe, and restrain'd by their Precepts; which, if they observe it, they shall ever find, are the lest obey'd by those who pretend the most to obtrude them upon others.

That this is Language which Women often hear is certain: And such a one as knows no reason for what she has been taught to believe, but has been reprov'd, perhaps, for demanding one, can very hardly avoid being perswaded that there is much appearance of Truth in this; whence she will soon come to conclude, that she has hitherto been in the wrong, if upon any scruple of Religion, she has not gratify'd her Inclination, in whatever she imagines might tend to make her Life more pleasing to her. And should a young Lady, thus dispos'd, find a Lover whom she thinks has a just value for all her good Qualities, which at best, perhaps, procure her but the cold Civility of her Husband, it is odds that she may be in danger of giving him cause to wish she had been better instructed, than may possibly suffice for her Salvation: Which, whatever happens, none can pronounce, may not be secur'd from the allowances due to so great Ignorance, or at least by any timely Repentance: Whilst Honour, if not intirely Ship-wrack'd, it is scarce reasonable to hope, should suffer no Diminution on such an occasion; the which, that Women the most vertuously dispos'd, may never be within distance of, will, in an Age like this, be best provided for by their being betimes instructed in the true Reasons and Measures of their Duty; since those, who are so, are not only better able to defend their Vertue, but have also the seldomest occasion for such a defence. Men, how ill soever inclin'd, being aw'd by, and made asham'd to attaque with so pittiful Arguments, as Vice admits of, such as they see are rationally Vertuous; whilst easy ignorance is look'd upon as a Prey expos'd to every bold Invader: And whatever Garb of Gravity or Modesty it is cloath'd withal, invites such very often, even where the Charms of the Person would not otherwise attract them.

But as such Men who think that the understanding of Religion is a thing needless to Women, do commonly much more believe all other rational Knowledge to be so; let us see how reasonably these same Men who willingly allow not to Ladies any employment of their Thoughts worthy of them as rational Creatures, do yet complain, that either Play is their daily and expensive pastime; or that they love not to be at home taking care of their Children, as did heretofore Ladies who were honour'd for their Vertue; but that an eternal round of idle Visits, the Park, Court, Play-houses and Musick Meetings, with all the costly Preparations to being seen in publick, do constantly take up their Time and their Thoughts. For how heavy an Accusation soever this, in itself, is, may it not justly be demanded of such Men as we have spoken of, what good they imagine Mothers who understand nothing that is fit for their Children to know, should procure to them by being much in their Company: And next, whether they indeed think it equitable to desire to confine Ladies to spend the best part of their Lives in the Society and company of little Children; when to play with them as a more entertaining sort of Monkeys or Parroquets, is all the pleasing Conversation that they are capable of having with them? For no other Delight can ignorant Women take in the Company of young Children; and if to desire this, is not equitable or just, must it not be concluded, that the greatest part of those, who make the above-mention'd Complaints, do really mean nothing else thereby, but, by a colourable and handsome pretence, to oblige their Wives, either to be less expensive, or to avoid, it may be, the occasions of gaining Admirers which may make them uneasy? Neither can such, possibly, be presum'd upon any Principle of Vertue, to disapprove those ways of anothers spending their Time, or Mony, which themselves will either upon no consideration forbear; or else do so only, from a preference of things as little, or yet less reasonable; as Drinking, Gaming, or Lew'd Company. Such Persons of both Sexes as These, are indeed but fit Scourges to chastise each others Folly; and they do so sufficiently, whilst either restraint on the one side begets unconquerable hatred and aversion; or else an equal indulgence puts all their Affairs into an intire confusion and disorder: Whence Want, mutual ill Will, Disobedience of Children, their

Extravagance, and all the ill effects of neglected Government, and bad Example follow; till they make such a Family a very Purgatory to every one who lives in it. And as the Original cause of all these mischiefs is Peoples not living like rational Creatures, but giving themselves up to the blind Conduct of their Desires and Appetites; so all who in any measure do thus, will accordingly, more or less, create vexation to each other, because it is impossible that they should ever be at ease, or contented in their own Minds.

There being then so very few reasonable People in the World, as are, that is to say, such who indeavour to live conformably to the Dictates of Reason, submitting their Passions and Appetites to the Government and Direction of that Faculty which God has given them to that end; what wonder can it be that so few are happy in a Marry'd Estate? And how little cause is there to charge their Infelicity, as often is done, upon this Condition, as if it were a necessary Consequence thereof?

The necessities of a Family very often, and the injustice of Parents sometimes, causes People to sacrifice their Inclinations, in this matter, to interest; which must needs make this State uneasy in the beginning to those who are otherways ever so much fitted to live well in such a Relation; yet scarce any vertuous and reasonable Man and Woman who are Husband and Wife, can know that it is both their Duty and Interest (as it is) reciprocally to make each other Happy without effectually doing so in a little time. But if no contrary Inclination obstruct this Felicity, a greater cannot certainly be propos'd, since Friendship has been allow'd by the wisest, most vertuous, and most generous Men of all Ages to be the solidest and sweetest pleasure in this World: And where can Friendship have so much advantage to arrive to, and be maintain'd in its Perfection, as where two Persons have inseparably one and the same Interest; and see themselves united, as it were, in their common Off-spring? All People, it is certain, have not a like fitness for, or relish of this pleasure of Friendship, which therefore, however preferable to others in the real advantages of it, cannot be equally valuable to all. But where there is mutually that predominant Disposition to vertuous Love, which is the Characteristick of the most excellent Minds, I think we cannot frame an Idea of so great Happiness to be found in any thing in this Life, as in a Marry'd State.

It seems therefore one of the worst Marks that can be of the Vice and Folly of any Age when Mariage is commonly contemn'd therein; since nothing can make it to be so but Mens Averseness to, or incapacity for those things which most distinguish them from Brutes, Vertue and Friendship.

But it were well if Mariage was not become a State almost as much fear'd by the Wise, as despis'd by Fools. Custom and silly Opinion, whose consequences yet are (for the most part) not imaginary, but real Evils, do usually make it by their best Friends thought adviseable for those of the Female Sex once to Marry; altho' the Risque which they therein run of being wretched, is yet much greater than that of Men; who (not having the same inducements from the hazard of their Reputation, or any uneasie dependance) are, from the examples of others Misfortunes, often deter'd from seeking Felicity in a condition wherein they so rarely see, or hear of any who find it; it being too true that one can frequent but little Company, or know the Story of but few Families, without hearing of the publick Divisions, and Discords of Marry'd People, or learning their private Discontents from their being in that state. But since the cause of such unhappiness lies only in the corruption of Manners, were that redress'd, there would need nothing more to bring *Mariage* into credit.

Vice and Ignorance, thus, we see, are the great Sources of those Miseries which Men suffer in every state. These, oftentimes, mingle Gall even in their sweetest Pleasures; and imbitter to them the wholesomest Delights. But what remedy hereto can be hop'd for, if rational Instruction and a well order'd Education of Youth, in respect of Vertue and Religion, can only (as has been said) rectify these Evils? For vicious and ignorant Parents are neither capable of this, or generally willing that their Children should be instructed or govern'd any other ways, than as themselves have been before them.

One might hence therefore, it may be, reasonably believe, that God reserves to himself, by some extraordinary interposition of his providence, that Reformation which we are assur'd, will some time be effected. But yet if all Persons, eminent by their Quality, who merit not to be rank'd among the Vicious and Ignorant, would give the Example, much would thereby be done towards the introducing of a general amendment: Since these could make a greater care of Education in the above-mention'd Respects, become, in some degree, Fashionable: And even a reasonable thing will not want Followers, if it be once thought the Fashion. We have seen also that Mothers, in regard of their Childrens Instruction, ought to take upon themselves, as their proper Business, a very great part in that concernment; and one would think that there were no inconsiderable number of Ladies amongst us, who might, with hopes of success, be address'd to, that they would indeavour to acquit themselves herein of their Duty. I mean all such as are unhappily Marry'd; for what so good Reparation can they find for the misfortune of having foolish and vicious Husbands, who neglect or treat them ill, as the having Children honour'd for their Vertue, and who shall honour and love them, not only as their Parents, but as those to whom they owe much more than their Being?

To perswade such whose Heads are full of Pleasure, and whose Hours pass gaily, to seek their satisfaction in things of which they have never yet had any tast, could not reasonably be thought other than a vain Attempt: But they who are wretched, one would think, should be easily prevail'd with to hearken to any Proposition, which brings but the least glimpse of Happiness to them; and were that tenderness of their Children, which ingages Mothers to do them all the good they can, less natural than it is to Vertuous Women, one would imagine, that when from these alone they must expect all their Felicity in this Life, they should readily contribute what is in their Power to the securing to themselves this only Blessing which they can propose; and which they cannot miss of, without the greatest increase imaginable to their present unhappiness: Childrens Ill-doing being an Affliction equal to the Joy of their doing well. Which must be an unspeakable one to such Parents as are conscious, that this is in great measure the Fruit and Effect of their right direction. Nor is there any thing which a vertuous Man or Woman does not think they owe, or is too much for them to return to those to whom they believe themselves indebted for their being such. How great a Felicity then may a Mother, unhappy in the Relation of a Wife, (by procuring to herself such Friends as these) lay up for her declining Age, which must otherwise be more miserable than her unfortunate Youth? And how much better would she employ her time in this care, than in the indulging to a weakness, very incident to tender Minds, which is to bemoan themselves, instead of casting about for Relief against their Afflictions, whereby they become but yet more soften'd to the Impressions of their Sorrow, and every day less able to support them?

They are usually (it is true) the most Vertuous Women who are the aptest to bear with immoderate Grief, the ill Humour, or unkindness of their Husbands: But it is pitty that such, who (in an Age wherein the contrary is too often practis'd) have more Vertue than to think of returning the Injuries they receive, should want so much Wit as not to repay unkindness, with a just contempt of it: But instead thereof, foolishly sacrifice their Lives, or the Comforts of them (which is our All in this World) to those who will not sacrifice the least inclination to their reasonable Satisfaction: And how much wiser and more becoming Christians would it be for such Ladies to reflect less upon what others owe to them, and more upon what they owe to themselves and their Children, than to abandon themselves, as too many do, to a fruitless Grief; which serves for nothing else, but to render them yet less agreeable to those whom they desire to please; and useless in the World: Diseases, and, in time, constant ill Health being the almost never failing Effects of a lasting Discontent upon such feeble Constitutions. But I take leave to say, that the fault of those who make others thus miserable, and the weakness of such who thus suffer their Minds to think under Adversity, are in a great measure both owing to one and the same Cause, *viz.* Ignorance of the true Rules and Measures of their Duty; whereby they would be taught to correct every excess; together with the want of such other Knowledge (suitable to the Capacity and Condition of the Person) as would both usefully and agreably employ their Time: This Knowledge, tho' not perhaps of a Nature immediately conducing to form, or rectify the Manners, yet doing so, in a great measure, by restraining or preventing the irregularities of them. For as ill natur'd and vicious Men, if they know but how pleasantly and profitably to employ those tedious hours which lye upon their Hands, would be generally less Vicious, and less ill Humour'd than they are; so Women of the most sensible Dispositions would not give up themselves to sorrow that is always hurtful, and sometimes dangerous both in their Honour and Salvation (excess of Tenderness, when abus'd, too often producing Hatred, and that Revenge) if they were not only very little inform'd as to what God requires of them; but also very Ignorant in regard of any kind of Ingenious Knowledge, whereby they might delightfully employ themselves, and divert those displeasing Thoughts which (otherwise) will incessantly Torment, and Prey upon their Minds. She who has no Inclinations unbecoming a Vertuous Woman, who prefers her Husbands Affection to all things in the World; and who can no longer find that pleasure in the ordinary Circle of Ladies Diversions, which perhaps, they gave her in her first Youth, is but very ill provided to bear Discontent where she proposes her greatest satisfaction, if she has nothing within her self which can afford her pleasure, independently upon others: Which is what none can lastingly have, without some improvement of their rational Faculties; since as Childhood, and Youth, wear off, the relish of those pleasures that are suited to them, do so too; on which account the most happy would not ill consult their advantage, if by contracting betimes a Love of Knowledge (which is ever fruitful in delight to those who have once a true taste of it) they provide in their Youth such a Source of Pleasure for their Old Age as Time will not dissipate, but improve; by rendring their Minds no less vigorous, and its Beauties yet more attracting, when the short Liv'd ones of their Faces are impair'd, and gone. Whilst those whose Youthful Time has been devoted to Vanities, or Trifles, Age does inevitably deliver over either to melancholy Repentance, or (at best) to the wearisome Languishings which attend a Life deprived of Desire and Enjoyment.

Now in the pursuit of that Pleasure which the exercise and improvement of the understanding gives, I see no Reason why it should not be thought that all Science lyes as open to a Lady as to a Man: And that there is none which she may not properly make her Study, according as she shall find her self best fited to succeed therein; or as is most agreeable to her Inclination: provided ever, that all such Knowledge as relates to her Duty, or is, any way, peculiarly proper to her Sex, and Condition, be principally, and in the first place her Care: For it is indeed very preposterous for a Woman to employ her Time in enquiries, or speculations not necessary for her, to the neglect of that for Ignorance whereof she will be guilty before God, or blameable in the Opinion of all Wise Men; And to do this, is plainly no less irrational and absurd, than for one destitute of necessary Cloathing, to lay out what should supply that want upon things meerly of Ornament. There is yet, methinks, no difference betwixt the Folly of such Learned Women, and that of Learned Men, who do the same thing, except that the one is the greater Rarity.

But it is not perhaps very seasonable to propose that Ladies should have any greater Accomplishments or Improvements of their Understandings than the well discharging of their Duty requires, till it is thought fit for them to have that: The advantages of which to Men themselves, and the necessity thereof to a right Education of their Children of both Sexes are too evident, when reflected upon, not to obtain Encouragement of so much Knowledge in Women from all who are Lovers of Vertue, were it not true that Conviction does not always operate. The Law of Fashion or Custom, is still to be obey'd, let Reason contradict it ever so much: And those bold Adventurers are look'd upon but as a sort of *Don Quixots*; whose Zeal for any Reformation puts them upon Combating generally receiv'd Opinions, or Practices; even tho' the Honour of their Maker be concern'd therein: Or (what is nearer to most) their own Private and Temporal Interests. I am sure that a just consideration of both these furnishes every one with very cogent inducements to make what opposition they can to Immorality, both by amending their own faults, and by indeavouring to prevail upon others to correct whatever has contributed to the making us a vicious People. For, not to say that it is a rational as well as Pious Fear that God by some signal Judgment upon such as have abus'd many Mercies, should make an example of them for the deterring of others, it is more certain (tho' usually less reflected upon) that it is no way necessary to the punishment of any Wicked Ungrateful Nation, that God should interpose, by some extraordinary act of his Providence, to inflict upon them the due Reward of their Disobedience, and Ingratitude: Since so fitly are all things dispos'd in their Original Constitution, and the order of Nature to the All-wise ends of their Maker, that (without his especial

Interposition in the case) the establish'd course of things does bring to pass the effects that he sees fit in respect of the Moral, as well as of the Natural World; nor scarcely can any People from the avenging Hand of the Almighty, in the most astonishing Judgments which can render them an eminent example of his Displeasure, receive any severer Chastisement, than what they will find in the Natural result and consequences of their Moral Corruption when grown to an Extremity.

It would be to enter into a large Field of Discourse to shew how experience has always attested this. And we perceive, but too sensibly, that Vice proportionably to its measure, carries along with it, its own Punishment, to need that we should search for Foreign, or Remote examples in proof hereof.

A general Contempt of Religion towards God: Want of Truth and Fidelity amongst Men: Luxury and Intemperance, follow'd with the neglect of industry, and application to useful Arts and Sciences, are necessarily attended with misery, and have been usually also, the Fore-runners of approaching Ruine to the best and most flourishing Governments which have been in the World. And as in the same proportion that these things do any where prevail, so must naturally the unhappiness of such a People; it is evident, that for any Prophane, Debauch'd, or Vicious Nation to expect a durable Prosperity, is no other than to hope that God will in their Favour (who have justly incur'd his Indignation) withhold the natural Effects of that Constitution and Order of things, which he has with infinite Wisdom Establish'd: A Conceit too contradictious to Reason, as well as too Presumptuous for any one, I suppose, to entertain.

FINIS.